Cambridge English for
Scientists

Tamzen Armer
Series Editor: Jeremy Day

CAMBRIDGE
UNIVERSITY PRESS

CAMBRIDGE
UNIVERSITY PRESS

University Printing House, Cambridge CB2 8BS, United Kingdom

Cambridge University Press is part of the University of Cambridge.

It furthers the University's mission by disseminating knowledge in the pursuit of education, learning and research at the highest international levels of excellence.

www.cambridge.org
Information on this title: www.cambridge.org/9780521154093

© Cambridge University Press 2011

First published 2011
6th printing 2014

Printed in Poland by Opolgraf

A catalogue record for this publication is available from the British Library

ISBN 978-0-521-1540-93 Student's Book with Audio CDs

Introduction

The aim of *Cambridge English for Scientists* is to improve your professional communication skills whether you are a professional or a student scientific researcher. To give you practice in carrying out the most common communication tasks of a researcher in English, each unit contains:

- situation-based activities so you can practise the language and communication skills you have learned in realistic contexts
- engaging topics based on examples of published scientific research
- realistic listening activities so you can learn the language you need to participate in meetings and discussions with colleagues and supervisors
- relevant vocabulary presented and practised in professional contexts

Audioscripts for the listening material and a complete answer key, including answers for some of the discussion questions and activities, are at the back of the book. You will also find a full glossary containing explanations of useful words and phrases common to all fields of scientific research as well as some of the more specialised words connected to the scientific research case studies explored in each unit. In addition, you can find extra activities online at www.cambridge.org/elt/englishforscientists

How to use *Cambridge English for Scientists* for self-study

If you are working on your own, you can do the units in any order you like. Choose the topic that you want to look at and work through the unit, doing the exercises and checking your answers in the answer key. Note any mistakes you make, and go back and listen or read again to help you understand what the problem was. For the listening exercises, it's better to listen more than once and to look at the audioscript after the exercise so that you can read the language you've just heard. For the speaking activities, think about what you would say in the situation. You could also try talking about the discussion points with your colleagues or friends.

I hope you enjoy using the course. If you have any comments on *Cambridge English for Scientists*, you can send an email to englishforscientists@cambridge.org

Tamzen Armer (BSc, CELTA, DELTA) graduated with a degree in Anatomical Sciences. Her professional experience as a scientific researcher includes a one-year placement at the Multiple Sclerosis Society laboratory at the Institute of Neurology, London, followed by a full-time position as a research assistant at the Christie Hospital, Manchester. As an English language teacher, she has taught in South Korea, the UK, New Zealand and most recently in Australia. She is currently the Assistant Director of Studies at the University of Canberra English Language Institute.

UNIT 1 Getting started in research

- Planning a career in science
- Applying for research funding
- Writing up a résumé or CV
- Preparing for an interview

Planning a career in science

1 a **In pairs, discuss the following questions.**

1 Why did you choose a career in science?
2 What field of science are you currently working or studying in?
3 What would you like to do next in your work or studies?

b **Many scientists continue their education in other countries. The table below summarises higher education for science in the US. Make a similar table for your country and then answer the following questions.**

1 Is science education in the US similar to science education in your country?
2 If you decided to study in the US, which qualification would be best for you?

Higher education for science in the US

Qualification (lowest to highest)	Category	Duration (full-time)	Place of study
Associate of Science degree (AS)	undergraduate	2 years	community college or junior college
Bachelor of Science degree (BS)	undergraduate	2 or 4 years*	college or university
Master of Science degree (MS)	graduate (postgraduate)	2 years	university or graduate school
Doctoral degree (PhD)	graduate (postgraduate)	3 to 8 years	university or graduate school

* Students who have already completed an Associate (AS) degree can become a Bachelor of Science if they study for two more years.

2 **a** ▶ 1.1 Eriko is from Japan and will soon complete a PhD in biotechnology in London. She is discussing the next stage in her career with her supervisor, Susana. Listen to part of their conversation and tick the options which interest her and put a cross next to the options which do not.

- ☐ teaching (undergraduate) students
- ☐ doing post-doctoral research
- ☐ supervising a research team
- ☐ finding a permanent position at a university
- ☐ discussing theory
- ☐ doing practical fieldwork
- ☐ staying in London
- ☐ finding a well-paid job

b ▶ 1.2 You will hear eight sentences from Eriko and Susana's conversation. Listen and complete the first row of the table by writing the number of each sentence (1–8) in the correct column.

Talking about ...			
likes or dislikes	past experiences	future (more certain)	future (possible)

c Look at the underlined phrases in Audioscript 1.2 on page 91. Put the underlined phrases into the correct part of the second row of the table in Exercise 2b.

3 **a** Think about your career in science and make notes on:
- what you enjoy most about working in your scientific field
- what you would like to do (and not like to do) next in your career
- which of your past and present experiences are most relevant to your future in science

b In pairs, take turns to interview your partner about his/her career path in science. Use the phrases from Exercise 2c to help you.

Applying for research funding

4 a Read the following extract from a website and then, in pairs, answer the questions below.

1 Can an organisation apply for this scholarship?
2 Would you be interested in applying for SARF? Why / why not?
3 What information might you need to include on your application form?
4 What are the advantages of attracting scientists 'with future potential for leadership in their field' to a country?

b Eriko has decided to apply to SARF and has downloaded an application form. Look at the list of sections on the form (1–10) and match each one to Eriko's notes on the information she needs to provide (a–j).

About

The Sheridan Australian Research Fellowship (SARF) aims to develop science in Australia by attracting outstanding scientists in their field to continue their research in an Australian university or research institution. SARF fellowships are awarded to individual scientists with future potential for leadership in their field. Successful applicants receive a 5-year grant covering salary, travel and relocation costs.

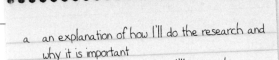

Sheridan Australian Research Fellowship SARF

APPLICATION FORM

1 APPLICANT
2 CURRENT APPOINTMENT AND ADDRESS
3 LOCATION OF PROPOSED STUDY
4 SPONSOR'S RECOMMENDATION
5 DEPARTMENTAL SUPPORT
6 PROJECT TITLE
7 PROJECT SUMMARY
8 DETAILS OF PROPOSED RESEARCH
9 BUDGET
10 NOMINATED REFEREE WITH PERSONAL KNOWLEDGE OF APPLICANT

a an explanation of how I'll do the research and why it is important
b a short description of what I'll research
c a statement from a senior researcher explaining why I'm a suitable applicant
d how much I plan to spend on my research
e the job I do now
f the name of someone to support my application
g what I'll call my research
h permission from my head of faculty to use his/ her resources
i where I plan to study
j my personal info

5 a Section 7 of the form asks applicants to write a project summary of their research proposal. Think about a research project in your area. In pairs, take turns to summarise the project following the instructions (1–6) below.

1 State the aims of your research
2 Define what the problem is
3 Explain why your topic is worth researching
4 Say what the expected outcomes of the research are
5 Outline the procedures you will follow
6 Outline how you will limit your investigation

b Read Eriko's completed project summary on page 9. Then say what you think the commercial applications of Eriko's research might be.

7 PROJECT SUMMARY

Provide a brief summary of aims, significance and expected outcomes of the research plan

A 3-D odour-compass for odour-detecting robots

Odour-sensing robots offer many benefits over the current use of animals in similar roles, including safety, efficiency and durability. **[A] However, the robots which have been developed to date are limited** by the fact that they can only accurately detect and navigate towards odour plumes if they are within direct 'sight' of the chemical source. Clearly, in real world situations, obstacles may well impede the robot's detection ability, and at present, odour-sensing robots are therefore only of limited use. **[B] The proposed research will concentrate on developing** a robot which is able to gather readings in three dimensions and therefore overcome the limitations of current models in odour-detection. **[C] This technology will make robots a more effective substitute for animals.**

[D] This research aims to develop existing robotic technology to create a three-dimensional (3-D) odour compass to be used as a navigation tool in searching for an odour source. **[E] This will then be tested experimentally** in simulated environments where wind direction is not stable or where obstacles interfere with odour distribution. A second stage in the research will be to develop the robot's environmental sensors, thus allowing it to safely negotiate the terrain to reach the source of the odour. **[F] This should produce a robot which is able to** both detect and move to the source of an odour, even on difficult terrain.

c Match each highlighted section in the summary (A–F) to the correct function (1–6) from the list in Exercise 5a.

d Look at the highlighted sections A–F again. Underline the words that you could use in your own project summary. Makes notes like the following example.

However, to date and *limited* to define the problem (A).

6

a Complete the project summary by another researcher below using the correct word or phrase from the box.

> aims to   however   the initial phase   the proposed research   the study   will indicate

Consumer interest in wines produced in organic vineyards has increased significantly in the last few years. (1) _____ , to date it is unclear whether these production methods actually improve soil or grape quality. (2) _____ will be the first phase of a long-term study on a New Zealand vineyard. These results (3) _____ whether methods of viticulture improve grape quality.

The research (4) _____ investigate the effects of organic agriculture on soil and grape quality. (5) _____ will consist of two treatments, organic and conventional (the control), each replicated four times in a randomised, complete block design. All organic practices will follow the standards set out by the Food Standards Australia New Zealand (FSANZ).

(6) _____ will assess soil quality using physical, chemical and biological indicators over six years. The next phase will then assess the physiology of the vines.

b Write a short project summary of about 150 words for the research you discussed in Exercise 5a above. Use the phrases you noted in Exercises 5d and 6a.

Writing up a résumé or CV

7 **a** **In pairs, discuss the following questions.**

1 Have you ever applied for a job in science? If not, what kind of job would you like to apply for in the future?

2 Which of the following documents are job applicants usually asked for in your country?
- application form
- biodata
- cover letter (covering letter)
- résumé or CV (curriculum vitae)

3 Have you ever written one of these documents in English?

4 Do you think that the information you include and the way you organise a résumé or CV in English will be the same as a résumé or CV in your own language?

b **Section 1 of the SARF application form asks applicants to include a copy of their CV. In pairs, look at the list of possible headings for a CV (a–l) and then answer the following questions.**

1 Would you use all the headings (**a–l**) on your CV? Why / why not?

2 How would you organise the information in your CV? Put the list of headings (**a–l**) in the best order.

3 What kind of information would you include under each heading? Make suggestions for each heading.

a ☐ computer skills		g ☐ publications	
b ☐ dissertations		h ☐ research experience	
c ☐ education		i ☐ study abroad	
d ☐ grants and awards		j ☐ teaching experience	
e ☐ personal information		k ☐ technical skills	
f ☐ presentations		l ☐ travel	

8 **a** ▶ **1.3 Eriko is getting advice from Susana about writing her CV. Use the list in Exercise 7b to complete the headings Eriko will use.**

- Personal Information
- (1) _____
- Research Experience
- Technical Skills
- (2) _____
- Publications
- (3) _____ and (4) _____
- Presentations

b **Look at Eriko's list in Exercise 8a and compare it with your ideas from Exercise 7b. Did you choose the same headings and put them in the same order as Eriko? If not, what is different?**

c ▶ **1.3 Listen to the conversation again. What TWO things does Susana say about how a CV should be organised?**

9 **a** **In pairs, look at an extract from the CV of a student, Carlos, on page 86. According to Susana's advice in Exercise 8c, does Carlos need to make any changes to what he has written?**

b When adding details to your CV, it is a good idea to use bullet points rather than full sentences. Look at the following revisions to another part of Carlos's CV and then answer the questions below.

~~One of my research focuses was~~ to examine the relationship between vegetation and the hydroperiod ~~by~~ producing detailed graphical profiles.

~~The research for my PhD focused on the analysis of~~ the intra- and inter-annual variability of perilagoonal vegetation.

* produced detailed graphical profiles to examine the relationship between vegetation and the hydroperiod

* analysed the intra- and inter-annual variability of perilagoonal vegetation

1 What kind of word comes first in each bullet point? How is this word formed?
2 Why does he move *to examine the relationship between vegetation and the hydroperiod* to the end of the first sentence?

C Rewrite the following sentences as bullet points.

1 My main research focus was to generate specific carbohydrate oligomers by using pure cloned enzymes.
2 During my project, I focused on the creation of a new CD4 positive HeLa cell clone.
3 As part of the Cell Wall Genomics team, I have developed sensitive methods to determine the fine structure of pectins in maize.
4 I have been involved in investigating the way the myocardium adapts following exercise, particularly the adaptation that takes place at the sub-cellular level.

10 a Your CV should always include any publications you have worked on in their correct citation form. In pairs, answer the following questions.

1 What is the correct order of information in a citation? Number the items in the box below in order from 1 to 6.

☐ page numbers ☐ journal volume and/or issue number
☐ title of article ☐ year ☐ journal name ☐ author's name

2 If the paper has not yet been published, what do you write instead of the *volume* and *page*?
3 If the paper has been submitted (given) to a journal but not yet accepted, what do you write instead of the *journal name*, *volume* and *page*?

b Write out the information for three different publications Carlos has worked on (1–3) in the correct citation form.

1 *Submitted manuscript.* / (2011) / Hernandez Sanchez, R. and Alvarez, C.M. / 'Salinity and intra-annual variability of perilagoonal vegetation'
2 Environmental Management Review / (2011) / 'Declining peri-dunal variability in Doñana' / *In press.* / Hernandez Sanchez, R., Gomez Herrera, S.A. / and Alvarez, C.M.
3 pp167–184 / 'Hydroperiod effects on peri-dunal vegetation' / Vol 2. / Spanish Hydrology Journal / (2010) / Hernandez Sanchez, R. and Alvarez, C.M.

11 Think about a job or a scholarship you would like to apply for and then write a <u>first draft</u> of your CV. Use the advice in Exercises 7 to 9 to help you.

Preparing for an interview

12 Read the extract of an email to Eriko from Dr Caroline Hansford of SARF and then answer the following questions.

1 How will Eriko be interviewed?
2 What does she have to do before the interview?
3 Why might this interview be particularly difficult?

13 a Eriko has decided to write her presentation and then to memorise it. In pairs, make a note of the advantages and disadvantages of:

* reading your presentation from a script
* memorising the script of your presentation
* not using a script (using notes only)

b ▶ 1.4 Eriko has asked Carlos to comment on her presentation. Listen to Eriko's first two attempts and answer the following questions.

1 How do you think Eriko feels?
2 What comment does Carlos make on her first attempt?

c What advice do you think Carlos might give to Eriko on her second attempt?

d ▶ 1.5 Listen to Carlos's feedback. Complete the notes below.

Good:
Remembered everything
Spoke more (1) _____
Speed OK
Practise more:
Make important words (2) _____ and
    (3) _____
Plan when to (4) _____
Practise (5) _____ words many times

Ask an (6) _____ (7) _____ to
    record your presentation so you can copy them.

e ▶ 1.6 Listen to Eriko practising the introduction to her presentation again.

1 Has she followed all of Carlos's advice?
2 Does the presentation sound better now?

and we plan to hold interviews in the final week of July. Your interview has been scheduled for Thursday 28 July at 0900GMT. As you are currently based in the UK, we will be interviewing you by conference call. Please write back to us to confirm your availability for this date and time.

We will be asking all interviewees to deliver a short presentation of their research proposal at interview. In your case, we would like to ask you to upload a video of yourself giving such a presentation no later than Wednesday 20 July.

f ▶ **1.7 Listen to the following extracts from the presentation and mark the stressed words with a (•) as in the example.**

1 Hello. My name is … and I'm currently …

2 My research focuses on …

3 This is useful because …

4 For example, …

5 However, there are a number of problems with …

g Complete the phrases in Exercise 13f with information that is true for you. Then practise saying the sentences, paying attention to stress and intonation.

h Imagine you are giving a short presentation like Eriko. *Either*: Choose a topic in your own research area and plan a short presentation (about 70 words). Plan where you will pause and which words you will stress, as in Exercise 13f. Then memorise the text. *Or*: Using the audioscript, memorise the beginning of Eriko's presentation. Then take turns to deliver your presentation to a partner. Give feedback on each other's presentations.

14 a Phone and video conferencing are both common for interviews and meetings nowadays. Complete the advice for interviews by conference call using the words and phrases in the box below.

application form   comfortable position   facing   late
phone number   questions   see   shuffle   thank   tone of voice

···························· **CONFERENCE CALL INTERVIEWS** ····························

Before your interview
- Find out exactly who you will be talking to
- Check whether they will be able to (1) _____ you or just hear you
- Check the date, time, the (2) _____ to dial in on, and the right code to access the conference call
- Read your CV and (3) _____ again
- Practise answering questions you might be asked
- Prepare (4) _____ to ask the interviewer

During your interview
- Don't be (5) _____ !
- Use your (6) _____ to sound confident and enthusiastic
- Do not (7) _____ papers (this will make a noise)
- Sit in a (8) _____ – do not move about too much
- Speak very clearly, (9) _____ the microphone
- When the interview is over, (10) _____ the interviewer(s) and end positively

b Look at the completed advice in Exercise 14a. Which do you think are the three best pieces of advice? Why?

15   Imagine you are being interviewed for a job or a fellowship. In pairs, make a list of questions which you might be asked. Then take turns to interview each other.

UNIT 2 The scientific community

- Communicating with scientific communities
- Writing a critical review
- Completing a Material Transfer Agreement

Communicating with scientific communities

1 a Match the methods of communication (1–6) to the pictures (a–f).

1 an academic journal
2 a conference
3 an online forum or science blog

4 a popular science magazine
5 a popular science book
6 a newspaper

b Which of these ways do you usually use to communicate?

c Why is it important for scientists to keep in touch with:

a other people in their field (e.g. biology)?
b people in their specialism (e.g. molecular biology)?
c people in other fields of science?

d In pairs, read the following statements and say which form(s) of communication from Exercise 1a the speakers should use to find the information they want.

1 I'm trying to learn more about the Hadron collider because it's big news, but it's not even close to my area so I'm finding the papers on it heavy-going.

2 At my university, I don't meet enough people in my field – I really need to network and build some connections with people working around the world.

3 I'm having a problem with one of my protocols. I've tried a few different things, but with no luck – I could do with some suggestions from other people of what to try next.

2 a Read the following five extracts and then say which form (or forms) of communication from Exercise 1a each one comes from. Which form(s) of communication are *not* included in these extracts?

A ... more people were pain-free when using the handheld device than those who had used an identical dummy device. Although the study by Lipton *et al.* (2010) has reliable results, there are some points to consider when putting these findings into context. Importantly, the results will need to be verified in larger trials that directly compare ...

B Tea and coffee drinkers have a lower risk of developing type 2 diabetes, a large body of evidence shows. And the protection may not be down to caffeine since decaf coffee has the greatest effect, say researchers in *Archives of Internal Medicine*. They looked at ...

C ... can be rapidly generated by lentivirus-mediated transgenesis. RNAi also holds great promise as a novel therapeutic approach. This report provides an insight into the current gene silencing techniques in mammalian systems.

D Hi! Has anyone had any experiences with nanoparticles sticking to glassware :−(? If so, does anyone know if there's a suitable silylation protocol to pre-treat the glassware to do something about this annoying non-specific adsorption? Thanks!

E Animal and *in vitro* studies suggest that aspirin may inhibit breast cancer metastasis. We studied whether aspirin use among women with breast cancer decreased their risk of death from breast cancer. This was a prospective observational study based on ...

b How easy was it to decide where extracts came from? How did you decide on the right answer?

3 a The language we use changes according to why we are writing (the purpose) and who we are writing for (the reader). It is important to notice the different styles of language used in English. Complete the second column of the table below, carefully reading the appropriate extract (A–E).

Feature	Examples	Extract
1 Asks the reader questions	Has anyone had ... ? _____	D D
2 Uses multi-word verbs (a verb with an adverb or a preposition)	_____ do something about	B D
3 Uses exclamation marks and emoticons	Hi! _____	D D
4 Uses non-specific references to the work of other researchers	_____	B
5 Uses specific references to the work of other researchers	_____	A
6 Uses impersonal phrases to avoid saying 'You' or 'We'	there are some points to consider _____	A E
7 Uses passive verbs to avoid saying who carries out a process	_____ can be rapidly generated	A C
8 Uses Latin language expressions	*et al.* _____	A E

b Which of the features in the table (1–8) are appropriate for formal for scientific research papers? Which are appropriate for personal communication (such as email)?

4 a In pairs, discuss the following questions.

1 When you have a problem at work, who do you usually ask for help?
2 Have you ever asked a question on a science internet forum? If so, was your question answered?

b Read three recent posts from an online forum (A–C) below. Imagine you belong to the forum where these questions are asked. Which questions could you answer? Which answers could you guess?

c Read the posts again. For each post, say which sentence or sentences (1–3) in each one the writer uses to:

a ask the question
b say what the problem is
c thank the reader

d How are the questions in the Subject field of each post different from normal questions?

e Think of a question related to your own research. Then write a three-sentence post for an online forum in an appropriate style using the phrases in the box to help you.

- Does anybody know what … is … ?
- I know that … , but I can't find / don't know …
- I was wondering how / what / why …
- I don't mean … , but …
- In other words, …
- Any help here would be appreciated.
- Thanks in advance.

5 In pairs, discuss the following questions.

1 What kinds of text do you need to write in English for your work or studies?
2 Why is it important to write your texts in an appropriate style?
3 What can you do to take note of the different styles of language used in English texts?

A
Subject: Filovirus Host Range?
....
(1) Does anybody know what the host range is for filoviruses (i.e. Ebola and Marburg)? (2) I know that they can infect most (all?) types of mammals and several species of birds, but I can't find the actual host range anywhere. (3) Any help here would be appreciated.

B
Subject: materials which x-rays can't pass through?
....
(1) I've been looking for a while now, but I can't find anything telling me what the radiopaque materials are. (2) In other words, which materials can't x-rays pass through? (3) Thanks in advance.

C
Subject: Quality of scientific writing considered in peer review?
....
(1) I was wondering how important the quality of the writing of a submitted paper is in the peer review process. (2) I don't mean the quality of the data, but the actual writing. (3) In other words, will a nicely written paper with the same data be more likely to be accepted?

Writing a critical review

6 **a** Read the headlines and beginnings of two news
articles reporting a recent scientific development.
Then answer the questions below.

> **The 'Chocolate Cure' For Emotional Stress**
> There may well be another important reason for
> giving your sweetheart sweets for Valentine's Day ...

> **New Evidence That Dark Chocolate Helps Ease Emotional Stress**
> The 'chocolate cure' for emotional stress is getting new support from a
> clinical trial published ...

1 Do you think the claims made in the headlines seem likely or unlikely? Why?
2 In general, how can the science reported in the media differ from the actual
science? Why do you think there is a difference?
3 If you wanted to learn more about the research you see reported in the
newspaper, where could you look for more information?

b Martina, a junior researcher, is supervising Ryuchi, an MSc Physiology
student. Martina has asked Ryuchi to investigate the claims in the
headlines and then to write a critical review of the research. Complete the
sentences below in your own words. Then in pairs, discuss your answers.

a If you read research *critically*, it means that you ...
b You should always read research critically because ...

7 **a** ▶ 2.1 Ryuchi has some questions about writing a critical review. In pairs,
discuss questions 1–5. Then listen and make notes on how Martina
answers the questions.

1 How long should my review be?
2 Can I write a critical review if I've only read the abstract?
3 How should I approach the reading? What should I read first?
4 Is it a good idea to think of questions I want answered?
5 Do I need to take notes or can I just highlight the relevant bits of the text?

b Before reading, Ryuchi writes seven questions to help him. Match the
questions (1–7) to the section of the research paper below where you
would expect to find the answer.

1 What variables were investigated?
2 How did the authors interpret the results?
3 What were the main findings?
4 Why is this research relevant?
5 Who/What was studied?
6 What procedure was used?
7 What was the hypothesis?

- **Introduction:** _____ _____
- **Method:** _____ _____ _____
- **Results:** _____
- **Discussion:** _____

c   Ryuchi has taken notes on the research paper that was reported in the news headlines in Exercise 6a. Use the glossary (pages 117–125 to check the meaning of the words in the box.

anxiety   assessment   classify   consumption   hormone   metabolic   microbiota
participant   trial period   urine

d   Read the Summary column. Which questions from Exercise 7b can you answer?

Reference: Martin, F-P.J., Rezzi, S., Pere-Trepat, E. et al. (2009). 'Metabolic effects of dark chocolate consumption on energy, gut microbiota, and stress-related metabolism in free-living subjects' J. Proteome Res, 8 (12), pp 5568–5579.

Section of paper	Summary	Opinion
Method:	• 30 young healthy adults • 40 g of dark chocolate/day x 14 days (20 g am, 20 g pm)	• small sample • (1) _____ trial period
	• pre-trial assessment of anxiety levels using questionnaires • participants classified as high or low anxiety	• using 2 groups further (2) _____ sample size
	• days 1, 8, 15 – blood and urine samples taken • analysed changes in cortisol and catecholamines in urine & energy metabolism and gut microbial activities	• didn't look at changes in (3) _____ levels or reported (4) _____ • No (5) _____ group • only young healthy participants
Results:	• reduction in stress hormones in the urine for all the participants • less difference between groups in energy metabolism and gut microbial activity	
Discussion:	• 40 g of dark chocolate a day for two weeks can change metabolism • could have long-term effects on health	• can't prove that (6) _____ caused the changes • need more people with the (7) _____ anxiety levels • give either chocolate or a (8) _____ • look at long-term stress, anxiety, health and (9) _____ changes • should use a (10) _____ trial

e   ▶ 2.2 Before writing his critical review, Ryuchi discusses his notes with Martina. Listen and complete the notes in the Opinion column, using one word from the recording for each answer.

f   From the information in Ryuchi's notes, discuss in pairs whether you think the research is:
   • credible?   • significant?
   • original?   • valid?
   • reliable?

8 **a** Read two extracts from Ryuchi's completed critical review and answer the questions.

1 Do the extracts include all the main points from Ryuchi's notes in Exercise 7d?
2 Which extract (A or B) …
a summarises part of the research?
b gives an evaluation?

> **A** 30 young healthy adults completed a pre-trial questionnaire to assess their anxiety levels and based on this, they were classified as either high or low anxiety. All participants ate 40 g of dark chocolate a day for 14 days. On days 1, 8 and 15 urine and <u>blood samples were taken</u> and <u>changes in</u> cortisol and catecholamines in the urine <u>were analysed</u>, as well as energy metabolism and gut microbial activity. <u>The research found</u> that after 14 days, the level of stress hormones in the urine was reduced in all participants. <u>In addition,</u> there was less difference between the two groups in energy metabolism and gut microbial activity.
>
> **B** <u>One problem with the research is</u> the small sample size (only 30 people) which was further divided into smaller groups. There was also no control group in the study, <u>making it impossible to</u> conclude that chocolate was the cause of the changes seen rather than some other factor such as other food or drink, lifestyle change or activity level. <u>Furthermore,</u> only young healthy adults were investigated and so <u>the results cannot be applied to</u> those who are older or have pre-existing health issues.

b Read the six extracts below from a critical review of another paper. Replace the underlined phrases with an underlined expression from Exercise 8a.

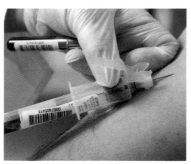  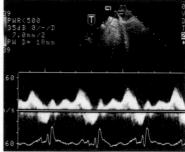

a *A bad thing about this research is* there were only 20 participants. *Another problem is* all the subjects were hospital employees.
b *Also*, the blood flow in the brachial artery was measured before they drank the coffee, and 30 and 60 minutes after.
c *The researchers looked at how the* blood flow *changed*.
d *The result of the research was* that the people who drank caffeinated coffee had decreased blood flow to their upper arm.
e *The results might not be the same for* the general population. There was also no measurement of the changes in blood pressure and blood flow after one hour, *so we can't* know when blood flow returns to normal.
f 20 subjects, between the ages of 25 and 50, who usually drank little coffee, were given either a caffeinated or decaffeinated Italian espresso coffee. *They gave blood* before the coffee was drunk, and an hour later.

c Put extracts a–f in the correct order to make two paragraphs. One paragraph should summarise part of the research, the other should give an evaluation.

9 Find a piece of published research you are interested in and then make a table like the one in Exercise 7d and take notes. Use your notes to write two paragraphs of a critical review in an appropriate style.

Completing a Material Transfer Agreement

10 a Read the beginning of the email sent to members of a laboratory. Then in pairs, answer the questions below.

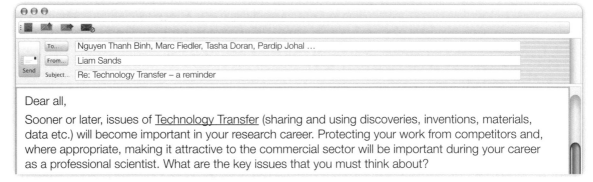

> To... Nguyen Thanh Binh, Marc Fiedler, Tasha Doran, Pardip Johal …
> From... Liam Sands
> Subject... Re: Technology Transfer – a reminder
>
> Dear all,
>
> Sooner or later, issues of <u>Technology Transfer</u> (sharing and using discoveries, inventions, materials, data etc.) will become important in your research career. Protecting your work from competitors and, where appropriate, making it attractive to the commercial sector will be important during your career as a professional scientist. What are the key issues that you must think about?

1 What is the purpose of the email?
2 What kind of discoveries, inventions, materials and data might you share with other scientists in your field?
3 What do you think are the key issues of technology transfer?

b The next part of the email identifies some key issues and offers advice on them. Match the headings (A–E) to the extracts (1–5).

A Huh??? What do I do now??
B Always read the small print!
C Look out! There may be a thief about!
D Your research is valuable – to others!
E Who, me?

> 1 _____
> Sooner or later someone in your field is going to ask you for some materials. Never send out any material without first checking if a Material Transfer Agreement (MTA) is needed.
> 2 _____
> Don't leave sensitive information, notebooks, etc. open on your desk or in unlocked rooms at the end of the day. You never know who might be in the building …
> 3 _____
> If you request materials from another lab, you will probably be asked for an MTA to sign. Not all MTAs are the same (some say 'we claim ownership of everything developed in your lab') so read carefully before signing and always ask if you're not sure.
> 4 _____
> Yes, you! Your research may have a commercial application. Always talk possible applications over with your supervisor or division head/director before you publish.
> 5 _____
> If you are still none the wiser, or unsure about any of the issues in this email, please talk to your group leader or contact me (Liam Sands) at the Technology Transfer Office.

C In pairs, discuss the following questions.

1 Does your place of work or study have similar rules to those in the email?
2 What kind of materials require an MTA?
3 What kind of information would you expect to be asked for in an MTA?

11 a Binh, a biochemist, is completing an MTA to receive some samples from a tissue bank in the UK. Read the MTA form on the right. Does this MTA ask for the kind of information you discussed in your answer to question 3 in Exercise 10c?

b ▶ 2.3 Binh's supervisor Alina is helping him to complete the MTA. Listen and complete Section A by circling the correct option (1–8).

c Binh has to write a brief lay summary of what the material will be used for in Section B of the MTA. In pairs, discuss the following questions.

1 What do you think a *lay summary* is?
2 What kind of language should Binh use or avoid when writing it?
3 Who will probably read the summary?
4 Why do you think the MTA asks for the summary to be written in this way?

MATERIAL TRANSFER FORM

SECTION A
(to be completed when **sending** or **receiving** material):

Recipient Researcher: Dr Alina Piotrowska

Recipient Institution & Address: School of Biological Sciences, University of the South, GPO Box 2010

Provider Researcher: Liverpool Tissue Bank

Material Name: Breast tissue microarrays – paraffin wax embedded tissue

Is this work involved with existing commercial arrangements?	(1) **Yes / No**
Does the work involving the material have commercial potential?	(2) **Yes / No**
Is this material hazardous?	(3) **Yes / No**
Is BioSafety Committee Approval required?	(4) **Yes / No**
Is Ethics Committee Approval required?	(5) **Yes / No**
If required, has Ethics and/or BioSafety Approval been received?	(6) **Yes / No**
Who will own the IP in any modifications to, or data collected on the material?	(7) **University / Other / Joint**
Will any University of the South students be involved in using the material?	(8) **Yes / No**

---

d Complete Binh's lay summary using the phrases in the box.

different types of   material is samples of
The aim of the research is to investigate
will be stained to show

12 Think of some material you often use in your lab. Write a brief lay summary of what the material is and what it will be used for, similar to the one Binh wrote in Exercise 11d.

SECTION B
(to be completed when **receiving** material):

Brief lay summary of what the material is and what it will be used for:

The (1) _____ human breast tissue, both normal and from (2) _____ tumour. The tissue (3) _____ expression of the Nek-2 protein, a protein which has been shown to be overexpressed in one class of tumours. (4) _____ Nek-2 expression in various tumour types and grades.

UNIT 3 Finding a direction for your research

- Doing a literature review
- Using evidence in arguing a point
- Taking part in a meeting

beetle

boxfish

termite mound

plant leaves

mosquito

snail shell

Doing a literature review

Biomimetics, or bionics, involves designing processes, substances, devices, or systems that imitate nature.

1 a Which natural phenomenon in the pictures above do you think inspired each of the following inventions?

1 air-conditioned buildings
2 body armour
3 super-aerodynamic car
4 painless hypodermic needle
5 harvesting water from fog
6 solar cells that follow the sun

b In pairs, discuss the following questions.

1 Can you think of any other biomimetic inventions?
2 Biomimetics groups are often multi-disciplinary, that is, they involve people from a number of different subject areas. What disciplines do you think might be included in a biomimetics group?

2 a Pia is a materials scientist. She would like to find a more efficient way of coating metallic bone implants with hydroxyapatite (HA), a bioactive calcium phosphate (CaP). Look at the diagram on the right. It shows a plasma-spray process for coating metallic bone implants with calcium phosphate. Use a dictionary to check the meaning of the words in the diagram.

b Pia has noticed a problem with the process shown in Exercise 2a, but she thinks that a biomimetic solution might be possible. In pairs, look at the diagram carefully and answer the following questions.

1 What do you think the problem might be?
2 Can you think of a biomimetic way to coat the implants with CaP? (Clue: think about how crystals grow naturally)

3 a Pia has decided to read up on the topic to help her plan her research to find a more efficient coating method. In pairs, discuss the following questions.

1 Why is it a good idea to review the literature before planning your experiment?
2 How can you find research papers which will be relevant to your area?
3 What might Pia's next step be after she has read some of the literature?

b Look at the extracts from the literature which Pia has found. Which extract(s) describe:

1 why CaP is used on metallic bone implants
2 the advantages of CaP-coated implants
3 the disadvantages of using plasma-spraying to CaP-coat metal

A
All coatings were found to undergo significant plasma-spraying-induced changes. Specifically, hydroxyapatite (HA) partly decomposed to α-TCP and tetra calcium phosphate. (Radin, S.R. and Ducheyne, P., 1992)

B
Uncemented HA-coated implants had better survival rates than the uncoated, cemented ones. (Havelin, L.I., Engesæter, L.B., Espehaug, B., Furnes, O., Lie, S.A. and Vollset, S.E., 2000)

C
Plasma-sprayed coatings have an irregular surface, and always contain some holes throughout their thickness. (Pilliar, R.M., 2005)

D
Surface engineering of biomaterials is aimed at modifying the biological responses while still maintaining the mechanical properties of the implant. Therefore, there has been research to develop CaP-based surface coatings on various metals for implant applications. (Paital, S.R. and Dahotre, N.B., 2009)

E
Since 1985, it has been reported that HA coatings on metallic implants can successfully enhance clinical success, and a less than 2% failure rate was reported during a mean follow-up study of 10 years. (Yang, Y., Kim, K-H. and Ong, J.L., 2005)

c Match the definitions (1–8) to the underlined words and phrases in Exercise 3b.

1 a further investigation into sth which happened before
2 a way in which sth can be used for a particular purpose
3 having parts of different forms, shapes or sizes
4 to cause sth to happen
5 to change
6 to continue to be sth or have sth
7 to decay or to break down into smaller parts
8 to improve the quality, amount or strength of sth

d Explain to a partner in your own words:

1 why CaP is used on metallic bone implants
2 two advantages of CaP-coated implants
3 two problems there are of using plasma-spraying to CaP-coat metal

e Pia has written a review of the literature she has found. Read the summary of her review below and then answer the questions.

1 Does Pia's summary include key information on why CaP coating is used on implants? Does it describe advantages and disadvantages of the process?
2 Has she used the same words as the original authors did in extracts A–E?
3 How does she refer to the work of other scientists?
4 What does *et al.* mean in 'Yang *et al.*, 2005'?

(1) The surface of metallic bone implants is often sprayed with calcium phosphates (CaPs) to improve the biological response (Yang *et al.*, 2005; Paital and Dahotre, 2009). (2) Studies have found better survival rates for coated implants (Havelin *et al.*, 2000). (3) However, the usual plasma-spray technique cannot coat all surfaces evenly (Pilliar, 2005). (4) In addition, the plasma-spraying process causes CaP input powders to break down into other compounds such as tetra calcium phosphate (Radin and Ducheyne, 1992).

f In a literature review, it is important to combine information from different sources and show how different pieces of information relate to each other. Look at Pia's summary again and answer the following question.

What word or phrase does Pia use to show that:
a there is a contrast between the information in Pilliar (2005) and Havelin *et al.* (2000)?
b Radin and Ducheyne's (1992) research shows another problem with spraying, different from Pilliar (2005)?

g Complete extracts 1–5 with the words in the box. There may be more than one possible answer.

As a result   In contrast   Moreover   On the other hand   Therefore

1 Kurella *et al.* (2006) used a continuous-wave Nd:YAG laser system to melt a CaP precursor on Ti–6Al–4V substrate. _____ , Paital *et al.* (2009) used a pulsed Nd:YAG laser system.

2 Coating crystallinity was observed to increase at higher temperatures. _____ , sputtered coatings heat-treated in the presence of water vapour at 450 °C resulted in a significant increase.

3 Thiriau *et al.* (2008) showed that the procedure results in more light-weight implants. _____ , Amrani & Guyton (2011) reported that surface damage in the CaP coating can also be observed.

4 A surface with a greater texture enhances cell interaction with complex tissue such as bone. _____ , creating three-dimensional features or textures on the surface of a biomaterial is becoming a reality.

5 Sliding and/or vibratory motions resulted in adhesion and cohesion at the interface of the two surfaces. _____ , adhesive damage caused bound particles to transfer from one surface to the other.

h The linking words in Exercises 3f and 3g show a relationship between two different sentences. We can also describe a similar relationship in a single sentence using the correct word *and* or *but*. Look at Pia's summary in Exercise 3e and:

- combine sentences (2) and (3) by replacing *However,* with *and* or *but*.
- combine sentences (3) and (4) by replacing *In addition,* with *and* or *but*.

i We can describe the relationships between sentences (2), (3) and (4) in Pia's summary in different ways. In pairs, look at the four ways below of organising the sentences and then decide which way (a–d) is best. Think about the style and the effect on the reader as well as the meaning of the sentences.

a *(Sentence 2)*. However, *(Sentence 3)*. In addition, *(Sentence 4)*.
b *(Sentence 2)*. However, *(Sentence 3)* and *(Sentence 4)*.
c *(Sentence 2)* but *(Sentence 3)*. In addition, *(Sentence 4)*.
d *(Sentence 2)* but *(Sentence 3)* and *(Sentence 4)*.

j Look at another extract from Pia's literature review. Complete the gaps with the linking words in the box. There is one word you do not need.

and   but   first   however   in addition   so

Biomimicry has been used to develop alternative coating techniques. (1) _____ , the metal is treated with strong base or acid (Kim *et al.*, 1996). This treatment transforms the surface into an alkali salt or hydrated oxide. These show negative surface charges, (2) _____ they can attract Ca^{2+} and cause CaP to grow on the implant. (3) _____ , a disadvantage of this method is that it can cause surface problems, (4) _____ these can affect the survival of the implants. (5) _____ , these methods cannot be used to coat stainless steel because its alkali salts and oxides do not show negative surface charges (Miyazaki *et al.*, 2000).

Using evidence in arguing a point

4 a Read the information about fog. In pairs, can you think of a way the properties of water can be used to capture water from fog?

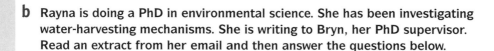

What is fog?

Fog develops in almost the same way as a cloud. However, fog actually touches the ground rather than being above it like a cloud. Fog is made up of tiny water droplets, which are usually around 10 μm in diameter. Fog forms when the air cools to a point where it can no longer hold all of the water vapour it contains (the dew point). The water vapour therefore condenses into tiny liquid water droplets, on surfaces such as the ground, roofs or around microscopic particles such as dust and pollutants in the air. The water droplets are hydrophilic, that is they attract other water droplets, and so once the process has begun, larger drops of water can form.

b Rayna is doing a PhD in environmental science. She has been investigating water-harvesting mechanisms. She is writing to Bryn, her PhD supervisor. Read an extract from her email and then answer the questions below.

> … wondering if I could arrange a meeting with you some time next week? I'd like to discuss an idea for a possible new direction to take our research in.
>
> Basically, I've been doing some reading on the Namib Desert Beetle and think that there might be a way to design some kind of water-harvesting material based on its wings.
>
> They are covered in hydrophilic bumps which attract water droplets in the fog. The drops get larger, and when they become too heavy to stay on the bump they roll off. The bumps are surrounded by hydrophobic channels so the water rolls down into the beetle's mouth.
>
> I really think it might be possible to develop a superhydrophobic material which has a surface covered in superhydrophilic bumps to trap water droplets in fog and this is what I'd like to …

1 What is the difference between *(super-)hydrophilic* and *(super-)hydrophobic*?
2 What does Rayna hope to design?
3 What is the biological inspiration for her design?
4 How does she plan to use this inspiration in her design?

c In pairs, draw a diagram of the design described in Rayna's email. Compare your diagram with the one in the key on page 106.

d ▶ 3.1 Listen to Rayna and Bryn's meeting. Is Bryn interested in Rayna's idea? Why / why not?

e ▶ 3.1 Listen again and answer the questions.

1 Why does Bryn think Rayna's idea is more complicated than the lotus-inspired design?
2 Why does Rayna think her material would be more efficient than the lotus-inspired design?
3 Why does Rayna think her material would be more effective than fog-catching nets?
4 What two uses does Rayna suggest for her material?
5 Which use is Bryn most interested in?

5 a When we are arguing with someone, we need to use evidence to support our point of view. We can use 'because' or 'because of' to give a reason or 'so' to show a result of a situation. Look at the following examples and then complete sentences 1–5 below using *because*, *because of* or *so*.

- I think nets must be less efficient **because** they have holes in them.
- I think nets must be less efficient **because of** the holes in them.
- They have holes in them, **so** I think nets must be less efficient.

1 _____ the wave of depolarisation running along the cell, a series of new action potentials is triggered.

2 _____ the magnitude of the energy loss is greater for phosphorescence than for fluorescence, phosphorescence occurs at longer wavelengths than fluorescence.

3 The internal dynamics of the proton are complicated _____ they are determined by the quarks exchanging gluons.

4 Root gravitropism influences the plant more than root hydrotropism, _____ hydrotropism is difficult to observe *in vivo*.

5 The remaining subjects were excluded from the analysis _____ missing data.

b ▶ 3.2 Listen to this extract from Rayna and Bryn's conversation and circle the phrase in bold that the speakers actually use. Check your answers in Audioscript 3.2 on page 93.

Rayna: <u>I think we could / We can</u> create a material which <u>will / could be used to</u> harvest water from fog.

Bryn: Yes, <u>that might be possible / we can</u>, but <u>it wouldn't be / I don't believe it would be</u> any better than the lotus-inspired surfaces Meera and Zein are working on.

Rayna: That's true, <u>but it seems to me that / but</u> this would be more efficient.

c Look at the alternatives in the sentences in Exercise 5b. The meanings are the same. Which version of the conversation is more polite? Why?

d Make the sentences below more polite by using the less certain and less direct kind of language in Exercise 5b.

1 I think that biomimetic solar panels which move with the sun can be created by using alternative materials and designs.

2 They will be useful in developing areas, where motor-based sun-tracking panels are not affordable.

3 Also, solar cells that track the sun are probably more efficient at generating power than those in a fixed position.

6 Think of an issue which people in your field often argue about. Then in pairs, argue for or against the point. Remember to use evidence to support your view and phrases to sound polite, as in Exercises 5a and 5b.

Taking part in a meeting

7 a In pairs, discuss the following questions.

1 Have you ever taken part in a meeting in English? If so, who was the meeting with and how was it?

2 What might be difficult about having a meeting in English, apart from the language difficulties you might have?

b ▶ 3.3 Listen to four scientists talking and take notes about problems they have had in meetings in English.

1 Sahal: _____

2 Hitomi: _____

3 Sam: _____

4 Radek: _____

c Have you ever had a problem like those described by the speakers?

8 a Sarah, Deepak and Ali work together as part of a team developing biomimetic adhesives by mimicking the way geckos stick to surfaces. Read the information below. Then in pairs, answer the following questions.

1 How does the physical structure of the gecko's foot help it to stick to surfaces?

2 How does the way the gecko places its foot help it to stick?

3 How do gecko toes become 'unstuck'?

4 Why does dirt not collect on the gecko's foot?

Geckos can easily run up a wall or across a ceiling because of their remarkable toes, which are made up of a hierarchy of structures that act together as a smart adhesive.

The pad of a gecko toe is crossed by many ridges or *scansors*, which are covered with small hair-like stalks called *setae*. Each foot can have up to about 2 million setae which cluster in diamond-shaped groups of 4. Each seta branches into hundreds of tiny endings with flattened tips. These tips are known as *spatulae*.

Many people have investigated just how geckos are able to stick and they have found that it is due to Van der Waals forces. These are attractive forces between molecules in the gecko feet and in the surface they stick to. To maximise the area available to create these forces, it is important that the setae are oriented correctly, as they are when the animal walks.

In their resting state, the setae bend proximally like a claw. When the gecko places its foot, the setae extend so that their tips point away from the body. The spatulae sit flat against the surface which sets up strong adhesive forces. The gecko also slides the foot very slightly creating a shear force. The ability of the gecko to stick is therefore not just because of the structure of the foot, but because of the whole locomotor system.

However, it is not only this sticking power which interests scientists. Because geckos can run up walls and across ceilings, they must be able to rapidly switch between sticking and detaching. They do this by changing the shape of the setae to increase the angle between seta and surface to more than 30 degrees, allowing the foot to be peeled away.

Gecko spatulae are also self-cleaning. Van der Waals forces form between the spatulae and pieces of dirt. However, because only a few spatulae can adhere to a single piece of dirt, when the dirt comes close to the surface the gecko is walking on, stronger forces pull the particle off the gecko's foot, which therefore becomes clean.

b ▶ 3.4 Sarah, Deepak and Ali are holding their monthly research meeting. Sarah is the team leader, Deepak is a senior research assistant and Ali is a junior research assistant. Listen to the beginning of the meeting and answer the questions.

1 What has Deepak been doing differently in his recent study?
2 What does Ali ask him about at the end of the conversation?

c In your opinion, is Ali's question at the end of this extract relevant or irrelevant to the discussion? Why?

d ▶ 3.5 Listen to the next part of the meeting. Is Ali satisfied with Deepak's answer to the question? How do you know?

e ▶ 3.6 Now listen to the final part of the meeting.

1 Is your answer to the questions in Exercise 8c still the same, or have you changed your mind?
2 Does Deepak think Ali's question was relevant? Why?

9 a During the meeting, Ali interrupts both Sarah and Deepak several times. Do you think it is appropriate for a junior scientist to interrupt and/or be critical of a senior colleague's ideas? Why / why not?

b When you want to interrupt someone, it is important to sound polite. Three ways you can do this are to use:

- *could* or *can* to make the interruption into a question.
- *sorry* to show the listener might not like what you're going to do.
- *just* to show that you are not going to talk for too long.

Look at Audioscripts 3.4–3.6 on pages 93–94. Which phrases does Ali use to interrupt?

10 a ▶ 3.7 Listen to five extracts from the conversation between Sarah, Deepak and Ali. Write one word or phrase in each space.

1 _____ , for a while, people thought it could be capillary, but now it seems it's mainly …
2 _____ you're clear on the adhesion mechanism now, Ali?
3 That's OK. _____ , so as I was saying, what I've been looking at (*fade out*) is the effect of the geometric …
4 _____ , because we now know that they are curved, we've …
5 _____ , could I jump in and …

b What is the function of these words and phrases? Can you find other examples of words with this function in Audioscripts 3.4–3.6 on pages 93–4?

11 Work in groups of three. Imagine you all work in the same department and are holding your regular meeting in which you all discuss your recent work. Role play the meeting. Take turns to present your current research, interrupting to ask questions where necessary.

UNIT 4 Designing an experiment

- Describing approaches to data collection
- Designing an experimental set-up
- Describing material phenomena and forces
- Making predictions of experimental results

Describing approaches to data collection

1 a The scientific method is a process in which experimental observations are used to answer questions. Complete the collocations for describing the stages in the scientific method using the words and phrases in the box.

> a hypothesis   an experiment (x2)   conclusions   data (x3)   the question

- ☐ analyse _____
- ☐ collect _____
- ☐ conduct (or run) _____
- ☑ define _____
- ☐ design _____
- ☐ draw _____
- ☐ form _____
- ☐ interpret _____

b Number the stages (1–8) in the order you would normally do them.

c Read this extract from a student website and check your answers to Exercise 1b.

> The scientific method is a process in which experimental observations are used to answer questions. Scientists use the scientific method to search for relationships between items. That is, experiments are designed so that one variable is changed and the effects of the change observed. While the exact methodologies used vary from field to field, the overall process is the same. First, the scientist must define the question – what exactly they are trying to find out. Next comes the formation of a hypothesis, which is an idea or explanation for a situation based on what is currently known. The next stage of the method is the design of an experiment which will allow this hypothesis to be tested. Usually a primary run of the experiment is conducted, and any changes to the experimental set-up made. In each experimental run, data collection takes place, followed by data analysis. Finally the data is interpreted and from this, the scientist is able to draw conclusions.

d Read the extract again to find the noun forms of the verbs in the box. Which word(s) in the box use(s) the same form for the verb and the noun?

> analyse   collect   design   explain   form   observe   relate   run   vary

2 a Below are the summaries of five experiments. Read each summary and then choose which word correctly completes the heading.

A proton may consist of *quarks* and *antiquarks*

1 *Practical* / *Theoretical* research
   Murray Gell-Mann and George Zweig proposed that particles such as protons and neutrons were not elementary particles, but instead were composed of combinations of quarks and antiquarks.

2 *Field* / *Laboratory* experiment
   Mark-and-recapture models were used to measure seasonal and habitat changes in house mouse densities on sub-Antarctic Marion Island.

3 *External* / *Internal* validity
   The students were carefully matched for social status, subject area, ethnicity, education level, parental smoking, and exposure to targeted advertising.

4 *Descriptive* / *Experimental* study
   The amount of soy products eaten by each participant was assessed at the start of the study. During the 30 years of the study, the women's incidence of breast cancer was recorded.

5 *Qualitative* / *Quantitative* research
   To investigate the effect of eating dark chocolate on stress levels, a blood sample was taken and the levels of stress hormones measured. After eating the chocolate, a second sample was taken and hormone levels measured again.

b In pairs, can you think of an example of an experiment which describes the alternative heading in 1–5 of Exercise 2a (for example, an experiment which is practical not theoretical)?

3 a Silvana is a research assistant working as part of a team investigating methods of storing hydrogen (H_2) for use as an energy source. In pairs, answer the following questions.

1 What do you think are the benefits of using hydrogen as an energy source?
2 In what situations or applications could hydrogen fuels be used?

b Hydrogen could be an ideal energy source, but is difficult to store. In pairs, look at three possible methods of hydrogen storage below and discuss what you think the advantages and disadvantages of each one might be.

a contained as a gas in a high-pressure tank
b condensed into a liquid and stored in a tank
c adsorbed onto a porous material

c ▶ 4.1 Silvana is talking to her supervisor Dominique about the next phase in her research. Listen and answer the following questions.

1 Which method of hydrogen storage from Exercise 3b do they discuss?
2 What property of carbon fibres does Silvana think is most important to her research?
3 How many possible variables do they discuss?
4 At the end of the conversation, how does Dominique suggest Silvana should begin this phase of her research?

d ▶ 4.1 **Listen to the conversation again and tick the variables Silvana agrees to investigate in the next phase of her research.**

☐ carbonisation temperature
☐ heating rate
☐ nitrogen flow rate
☐ type of hydroxide – potassium (KOH) or sodium (NaOH)
☐ ratio of KOH or NaOH to carbon fibres

e **What reasons did Dominique give for *not* investigating all the possible variables? Do you agree with her?**

f **Complete the following summary on variables using the words in the box.**

> affects   collecting   controlled   data   dependent   independent

How much a variable (1) _____ a relationship can be discovered by (2) _____ experimental (3) _____ on changes to the relationship as the variable is changed. In an experiment, there will be:

- one (4) _____ variable – this is the feature you are measuring
- one or more (5) _____ variables – these are the variables which you change
- one or more (6) _____ variables – these are not being tested and so they stay the same.

g **Silvana wants to investigate the effect of the different hydroxides (NaOH or KOH) on hydrogen adsorption in the carbon fibres.**

1 In this investigation, which of the variables in Exercise 3d will be independent and which controlled?
2 What will be the dependent variable?

4 a **Look at the extracts (a–f) from Silvana and Dominique's discussion. Then answer the questions below.**

a <u>Maybe</u> you <u>could</u> **look** at the adsorption of hydrogen.
b <u>Perhaps</u> I <u>should</u> **look** at the 1273 K and 973 K temperatures.
c I <u>could</u> **make** different ratios of hydroxide to carbon fibres another variable.
d <u>Perhaps</u> I <u>could</u> **start** with looking just at a couple of different ratios.
e You <u>might</u> **be able to** just look at the papers you mentioned.
f <u>Maybe</u> I'<u>ll</u> **have** a talk to Mauritz about the adsorption protocols he's been using.

1 Do these sentences refer to the present or the future?
2 Are they used to discuss plans or suggestions?
3 What parts of speech are the underlined words?
4 What part of speech are the words in bold?

b **In pairs, role play a discussion between a researcher and a supervisor about the effect of temperature and rainfall on the population of the mosquito *Aedes albopictus*. First, decide which type of experiment (from Exercise 2a) should be used to investigate the effects. Then discuss what the variables in the experiment might be. Use the language you studied in Exercise 4a to help you.**

The Mosquito *Aedes albopticus*

Designing an experimental set-up

5 **a** **Match the instruments (1–8) to the pictures (a–h).**

1 calipers	3 geiger counter	5 litmus paper	7 seismograph
2 dynamometer	4 interferometer	6 oscilloscope	8 spectrometer

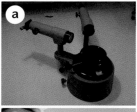
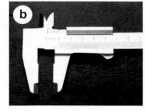
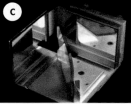

b **What meaning do the following suffixes add to the words in Exercise 5a?**

    -graph   -meter   -scope

c ▶ **4.2 Match an instrument in Exercise 5a to what it measures. Then listen to the conversations and check your answers.**

    pH   radiation   changes in voltage over time   light intensity   distance   torque
    motion   wavelengths of light

d **Do you take measurements as part of your research? What do you measure? What instruments do you use?**

6 **a** **Silvana is going to discuss her design for an experimental set-up with Mauritz, a more experienced researcher. In pairs, look carefully at Silvana's diagram and notes. Then discuss what words you think might complete the gaps (a–h).**

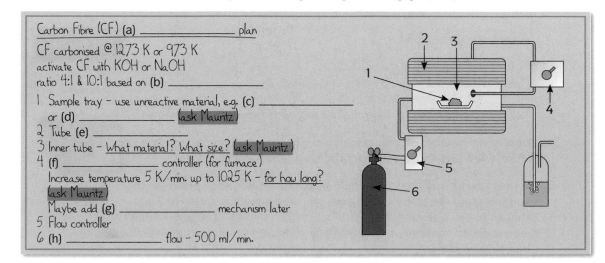

b ▶ 4.3 Listen to Silvana and Mauritz talking. Complete each space in Silvana's notes using one word from their conversation.

7 a Match the beginnings (1–7) to the endings (a–g) of some of Silvana's sentences from the conversation. Then look at Audioscript 4.3 on page 95 to check your answers.

1 I'm going to	a have the sample on a tray in an inner tube.
2 I was thinking of	b simply mixing the fibres with the hydroxides in pellet form, at the relevant ratios.
3 I think I'll try	c relying on natural convection first.
4 I thought I should	d running it through at 500 ml a minute, through the entire heat treatment.
5 I'm planning to	e start off with fibres which have been carbonised at two different temperatures.
6 I'll try	f stick with that.
7 I was planning on	g using those quantities first.

b Phrases 1–7 in Exercise 7a can all be used to discuss future plans. In pairs, answer the following questions.

1 Which phrases can we use to sound more confident about a future plan? Which are used to sound more tentative (i.e. less confident, more cautious)? Divide the phrases into two groups (more confident and more tentative).

2 Which phrases are followed by the INFINITIVE? Which are followed by a VERB-*ing* form?

8 a ▶ 4.4 In her notes in Exercise 6a, Silvana had four questions for Mauritz. Listen to an extract from the conversation and answer the questions.

> Sample tray: ceramic or steel?
>   Use (1) _____
> Inner tube: what material? Use (2) _____
>   what size? length (3) _____ m/diameter _____ cm
> Keep temperature constant for (4) _____ minutes

b Look at the responses Mauritz gives Silvana. Put a verb from the box into the space in each sentence. What is the function of these sentences?

don't   think   were   would

1 If I _____ you, I'd use steel.
2 Why _____ you try that to start with?
3 I _____ use less than 10 cm.
4 I _____ you should maintain the temperature for 75 minutes.

9 a Think of an experiment you are planning to do or would like to do in the future. Draw and label a sketch of the set-up as you plan it.

b Work in pairs. Student A, use your sketch to explain your plans for the experimental set-up. Try to use some of the phrases in Exercise 7a. Student B, ask questions for clarification (be sure to interrupt politely) and make suggestions if you can. Try to use some of the phrases in Exercise 8b. Then change roles.

Describing material phenomena and forces

10 **a** Complete the table below using the extract from the following research paper to help you.

> A promising candidate among the different adsorbent materials are activated carbons. Through activation, highly porous materials can be prepared. Due to their high porosity, activated carbon materials are able to adsorb large amounts of hydrogen. Following adsorption, hydrogen molecules can be found at two possible locations: (i) on the surface of the adsorbent, or (ii) as a compressed gas in the void space between adsorbent particles.
> adapted from Konowsky *et al.* 2009

noun	verb	adjective
compression	compress	
	adsorb	
	activate	
		porous

b In pairs, answer the following questions.

1 What noun suffixes are used in the words in the table? Can you think of other words with these suffixes?
2 What adjective suffixes are used in the words? Can you think of other words with these suffixes?
3 Why is it useful to know the suffixes for different parts of speech?

c The gapped words below all describe physical or chemical properties of substances. The meaning of each word is given on the right. Complete the words with the correct vowels (a, e, i, o, u).

1 br_ttl_n_ss	how easily something can be broken
2 c_p_c_t_nc_	how well something holds an electrical charge
3 c_nc_ntr_t_ _n	how much of one substance is found in another
4 c_nd_ct_v_ty	how well something allows heat or electricity to go through it
5 d_ns_ty	how much mass a given volume of a substance has
6 fl_mm_b_l_ty	how easily something burns
7 l_m_n_nc_	how much light passes through or comes from a substance
8 m_ss	how much matter is in a solid object or in any volume of liquid or gas
9 p_rm_ _b_l_ty	how easily gases or liquids go through a substance
10 p_r_s_ty	how many small holes are in a substance
11 pr_ss_r_	how much force a liquid or gas produces when it presses against an area
12 r_ _ct_v_ty	how easily a chemical substance reacts
13 s_l_b_l_ty	how easily something can be dissolved to form a solution
14 v_l_c_ty	how quickly an object is travelling
15 v_sc_s_ty	how thick a liquid is
16 v_l_m_	how much space is contained within an object or solid shape

d In pairs, answer the following questions.

1 Which is more **reactive**, aluminium or gold?
2 Which is more **brittle**, glass or steel?
3 Which is more **luminescent**, copper or neon?
4 Which is more **dense**, hydrogen or oxygen?
5 Which is more **flammable**, ethanol or water?
6 Which is more **viscous**, blood or water?

e Look at the adjectives in bold in Exercise 10d and the related noun forms in Exercise 10c. Divide the suffixes in the box below into those which usually indicate a noun form and those which are used in adjective forms.

-able -ance -bility -ent -ity -ive -ness -osity -ous -tion

noun suffixes: _____
adjective suffixes: _____

f In pairs, mark the following statements true (T) or false (F).

1 To **concentrate** a solution, add more solvent. To dilute it, add more solute. _____

2 Copper **conducts** heat better than aluminium. _____
3 Silver salts do not **dissolve** well in water. _____
4 Water can **permeate** limestone more easily than it can granite. _____

g Match the verbs in bold in Exercise 10f to the correct noun forms in Exercise 10c.

h Choose the correct word to complete the sentences.

1 It is possible to **extraction/extract/extracted** hydrogen from a widespread source – water.
2 A dye appears coloured because its molecules **absorb/absorbent/absorption** light from a part of the visible spectrum.
3 Pewter is an alloy of usually 80% tin and 20% lead. Adding the lead gives the alloy a blueish tinge and increases the **malleability/malleable**.
4 In the near-infrared waveband the **reflective/reflect/reflectivity** of water drops to almost zero.
5 New analyses on Antarctic samples have found no **detect/detectable/detection** iridium imprint above background due to cosmic dust.

11 Think of three different materials you often use in your research. Explain to a partner the physical or chemical properties of the materials and how you use them in your research.

Making predictions of experimental results

12 a ▶ 4.5 Silvana is about to start running her experiment. She is discussing possible results with Dominique. Listen to the conversation and say which of the three variables below Silvana thinks will *not* improve H_2 adsorption.

- carbonisation temperatures
- ratio of hydroxide to carbon fibres
- the type of hydroxide (KOH or NaOH)

b ▶ 4.5 Complete Silvana's predictions from the conversation using the words and phrases in the box. Then listen again to check your answers.

allow   any   between   expect   If   lead to   more   My prediction is that   will probably

a (1) _____ lower temperatures increase porosity, the fibres which are carbonised at lower temperatures (2) _____ adsorb (3) _____ hydrogen.
b I really don't (4) _____ there to be (5) _____ difference (6) _____ the sodium and potassium hydroxides.
c (7) _____ the higher ratio will (8) _____ better activation of the fibres and I think better activation will (9) _____ more adsorption.

13 **a** Sentences like prediction (a) in Exercise 12b are useful for talking about the relationship between a possible situation and the expected result of that situation. Read the following sentence and then answer the questions below.

If/When the fibres are more porous, they adsorb more hydrogen.

1 Which part of the sentence tells us about a possible situation?
2 Which part tells us about the result of that situation?
3 Can you rewrite the sentence with 'Fibres' as the first word?

b Now look at four more sentences and answer the questions which follow.

a If/When the fibres are more porous, they **adsorb** more hydrogen.
b If the fibres are more porous, they **will adsorb** more hydrogen.
c If the fibres are more porous, they **will probably adsorb** more hydrogen.
d If the fibres are more porous, they **might adsorb** more hydrogen.

1 What is the difference in meaning between:
   a sentences **a** and **b**?   b sentences **b** and **c**?   c sentences **b** and **d**?
2 Does the tense of verb change in the *if*-clause in sentences a–d?

14 Look at the description of the experiment below. Note down your predictions about what will happen at each stage.

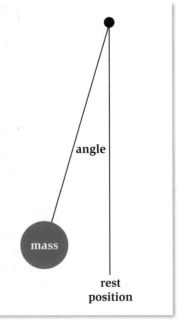

angle

mass

rest position

1 Hang a 1 m length of string to a fixed point. Tie a weight to the end. Pull the string back to the release point (a 45° angle) and time how long it takes to swing forward and back 5 times. Add a second weight and repeat. Make sure the release point is the same.

Prediction: _____

2 Pull the string back to an angle of 90°. Release and time how long it takes for 5 swings. Change the release angle to 20° and repeat. Make sure the weight used is the same.

Prediction: _____

3 Shorten the string to ⅔ of its original length. Pull the string back to 45°. Release and time how long it takes for 5 swings. Shorten the string again to ⅓ of its original length and repeat. Make sure the weight and release angle are the same.

Prediction: _____

15 Look back at the experimental set-up you sketched in Exercise 9a. Make notes on your predictions of what will happen in the experiment. Then, explain your predictions to a partner.

UNIT 5 Describing an experiment

- Describing a process
- Evaluating the results of an experiment
- Describing problems with an experiment
- Keeping a lab notebook

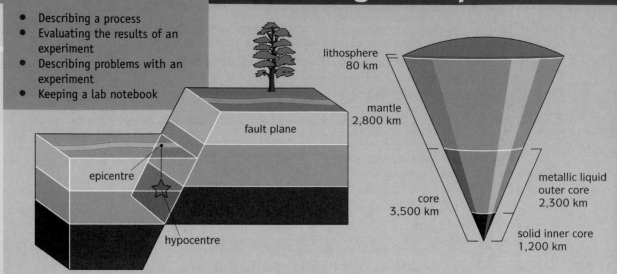

Describing a process

1 **In pairs, discuss the following questions.**

1 What processes do you need to describe in your field of research? Who do you describe them for?
2 How much detail do you need to include in your descriptions?
3 What do you think are the most important points to remember when describing a process for other scientists?

2 a Chuyu is researching seismicity (earthquake activity). In pairs, answer the following questions. Use the diagrams above to help you.

1 Do you know what causes earthquakes?
2 How might the Earth's mantle be involved in seismicity?

b Chuyu is investigating how the strength of different minerals in the Earth's mantle changes at high pressure and temperature, and how this relates to seismicity. Look at the sketch below of the process he uses to measure mineral strength. Using the diagram, can you describe the process in your own words?

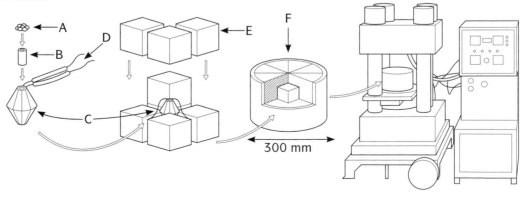

C Read Chuyu's summary of his procedure below. Then read the first paragraph again and say what labels A–F in the diagram represent.

(1) Multi-anvil high pressure apparatus <u>was used</u> to generate the high pressure and temperature for the specimen. (2) The powdered mineral sample was placed into a tube of rolled rhenium. (3) The rhenium tube was loaded into a ceramic octahedron. (4) Two tungsten-rhenium thermocouple leads were attached to the octahedron. (5) The octahedron was surrounded by a set of eight tungsten carbide cubes. (6) The cubes were placed into the space formed by six secondary anvils in the press.

(7) The press was pumped up to the correct pressure. (8) The anvils transform the directed force of the hydraulic press to hydrostatic pressure on the sample. (9) Heating of the tube was carried out using an electrical current conducted through the anvils. (10) Temperature was controlled with a programmable temperature controller. (11) Energy diffraction patterns were collected using a germanium solid state detector. (12) The patterns were analysed to work out the material's strength.

3 a Underline the main verb in each sentence of the summary in Exercise 2c (the first one has been done for you). Then answer the following questions.

1 Which main verb form is used in almost all the sentences?
2 How is this structure formed?
3 Why is this structure often used in describing a process?
4 Which main verb is different? Why?

b When you are reading the scientific literature, it is useful to record any VERB + PREPOSITION combinations you find. Read the summary again and find at least five VERB + PREPOSITION combinations.

c Complete the sentences by choosing the correct preposition (a, b or c).

1 First, leucine **was separated** _____ other amino acids in the protein hydrolysate.
   a for   b from   c with
2 Many bacteria, such as *Bacillus* spp., **can be isolated** _____ insects.
   a from   b to   c with
3 Subsequently, the specimens **were embedded** _____ methylmethacrylate.
   a at   b in   c to
4 The sections **were stained** _____ uranylacetate and lead citrate solutions.
   a with   b to   c under
5 MIP-1 β was added to wells which **had been coated** _____ BSA.
   a by   b from   c with
6 pH **is maintained** _____ 6.5, using Waterlife Buffer and Sera pH Minus.
   a at   b in   c to

4 a Chuyu has asked a colleague, Thabo, to check his work. Look at the summary in Exercise 2c again. Has it been written in an appropriate style? Would you change anything?

b ▶ 5.1 Listen to Chuyu and Thabo's conversation. What two changes does Thabo recommend?

c ▶ 5.2 Listen to the end of the conversation again and follow Thabo's instructions to combine the two sentences below.

The powdered mineral sample was placed into a tube of rolled rhenium. The rhenium tube was loaded into a ceramic octahedron.

d Which word (or words) does Thabo suggest replacing in the second sentence? What word replaces it (them)?

e Combine sentences 4 and 5, and then 6 and 7 in Chuyu's summary using *which* and *then*. Then compare your answers with the key on page 109.

5 a Look at the diagram from a review of supercritical fluid technology. Complete the description of the process using the words in the box.

> at   first   then   was   which [x2]

The diagram provides a schematic view of the rapid expansion of supercritical solutions (RESS) process. (1) _____ , the supercritical fluid (SF) (2) _____ pumped into the vessel (3) _____ contained the solid solute. The SF dissolved and became saturated with the solute. The resultant solution was (4) _____ introduced into a precipitation chamber by expansion through a laser-drilled nozzle. The precipitation unit was maintained (5) _____ conditions where the solute had low solubility in the SF. As the SF expanded, its solubility decreased, (6) _____ resulted in a high degree of solute supersaturation and subsequent precipitation.

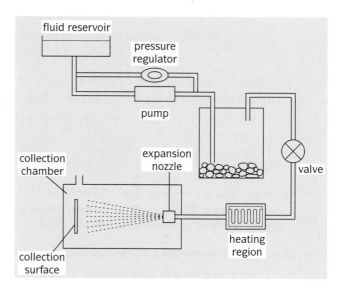

b Think of a process you know well. Draw a sketch and write a short description.

Evaluating the results of an experiment

6 a Think about an experiment you have done recently. Then in pairs, discuss 1–5.

1 Briefly describe the experimental process.
2 Explain what you predicted would happen.
3 Describe what actually happened.
4 Explain what you learned from the experiment.
5 Explain what you did as a follow-up to the experiment.

b Chuyu has carried out the procedure he described in Exercise 2c using the minerals olivine, ringwoodite and wadsleyite (all $(Mg,Fe)_2SiO_4$), and perovskite $(CaTiO_3)$ as samples. Look at the predictions he made before running his experiment. Use the glossary (pages 117–125) to check the meaning of the underlined words.

c ▶ 5.3 Chuyu is discussing the results with Lucia, a colleague. Listen to the first part of their conversation and mark each of Chuyu's predictions with a tick if it was right or a cross if it was wrong.

d ▶ 5.4 Listen to the next part of the conversation and answer the following questions.

1 What <u>two</u> things does Chuyu say he needs to do in the next experimental run to verify his results?
2 What other explanation does Chuyu give for the results?

- <u>differential stress</u> in the olivine and perovskite samples will go up with pressure
- perovskite will be stronger than olivine, i.e. it will <u>yield</u> later
- for olivine, increasing the temperature will reduce <u>yield strength</u>
- for perovskite, increasing the temperature will reduce yield strength

7 a ▶ 5.3 Chuyu and Lucia talk about their expectations of the results compared with what actually happened. Complete the extracts below using one word in each gap. Then listen to the first part of the conversation again and check your answers.

1 Right, well, firstly **I thought** _____ the differential stress in all of the samples _____ **go up** as the pressure increased, and **it** _____ for olivine and for perovskite.
2 Right. And, _____ **I expected**, the perovskite was the strongest. It yielded later than olivine.
3 OK, well, **I expected** _____ increasing the temperature _____ **reduce** yield strength.
4 Right. And **that's what** _____ **happen** with the olivine.
5 Really? **I** _____ **the minerals** _____ **all be affected** by temperature.

b Complete the following table using the expressions in bold in Exercise 7a. Then answer the questions below.

Expectations	Outcomes

1 Look at the phrases in the first column. Why do the speakers use 'would' in these expressions?
2 Why do you think Chuyu says 'That's what <u>did</u> happen' (not 'That's what happened')?

8 a Read the summary of Chuyu's most recent results. Match the highlighted parts of the summary to an underlined expression with a similar meaning in Audioscript 5.3 on page 96. (The tenses in the Audioscript may not be the same as in the summary.)

b Why do you think Chuyu uses different words in the written summary from those he used in the conversation with Lucia?

c In 1–4 below, each (a) sentence is from an informal conversation and each (b) sentence is from a formal research paper. Complete each (b) sentence using part or all of the highlighted phrases in Exercise 8a, and any other necessary words.

To date, strengths at high temperature and pressure of the upper mantle mineral olivine and the lower mantle mineral perovskite have been investigated. In addition, some research has been carried out on wadsleyite from the transition zone. In all three mineral samples, at ambient temperature, differential stress increased with pressure until yielding occurred. Of the minerals studied, perovskite has the highest strength and olivine the lowest. Olivine and wadsleyite have similar characteristics of yield strength in response to temperature; strength decreases significantly as temperature increases. Perovskite, on the other hand, shows no change in yield strength in response to temperature up to 873 K when temperature is increased at a pressure of 20 GPa.

1 a And then I've started looking at the petrography, too.
   b _____ , petrography studies have been
      _____ .

2 a As I expected, sodic glasses had lots of cations with low average field strength and non-sodic glasses didn't have many at all.
   b Sodic glasses contained _____ number of cations with low average field strength and non-sodic glasses the lowest.

3 a I thought the Al_2O_3 in the samples would decrease as SiO_2 increased, and it did.
   b In all five tephra samples, Al_2O_3 decreased _____ the increase in SiO_2.

4 a So far, I've looked at the morphology and mineralogy of tephra samples from La Malinche.
   b _____ , the morphology and mineralogy of tephra samples from La Malinche _____ examined.

9 Think about the experiment you discussed in Exercise 6a. Then write a short summary in a formal style using the text in Exercise 8a as a model.

Describing problems with an experiment

10 Think about an experiment you did where you had a problem. Tell your partner:
- what the problem was
- what the possible causes of the problem were
- how you discovered what was causing the problem
- how you solved the problem

11 a ▶ 5.5 Chuyu has been continuing his experiments using wadsleyite and has moved on to look at the fourth mineral, ringwoodite. He is talking to Lucia about some problems he has had. Listen and complete the second column of the table with the two possible causes of the problem.

Problem	Possible cause	Likelihood	Action to be taken
Expects ringwoodite to act like wadsleyite, but it doesn't.	1	likely/possible/ unlikely	Send sample for analysis
	2	likely/possible/ unlikely	Be more careful between runs

b ▶ 5.5 Listen again. How likely do they think each possible cause is? Circle the correct option in the third column of the table.

12 a Look at the phrases (1–5) below from the conversation. Which phrase is used to describe

  a a problem?
  b a possible cause?
  c the likelihood of something being correct?

  1 ... so far the results are **all over the place**.
  2 **It looks like** you're using olivine again.
  3 Yeah, **it's possible**. But **I really think it's unlikely**.
  4 **I guess** if my measurements aren't coming from the same base point then **there could be** problems.
  5 ... a calibration issue **is a possibility**.

b In pairs, think about a problem you are having with your current research. Use the expressions in Exercise 12a to describe some possible causes for the problem. Then explain how likely you think each one is.

13 a Chuyu has summarised his recent problems in a report for his supervisor. Complete the summary using the words in the box.

> appears   likely   possibility   possible   possibly   similar   surprising   unlikely

(a) *Because / Because of* the results obtained with wadsleyite, those from studies of ringwoodite are rather (1) _____ . Ringwoodite, like wadsleyite, is a transition zone mineral. (b) *So / As a result*, these minerals would be expected to act in a (2) _____ way. (c) *However, / But* in the current data, ringwoodite (3) _____ to behave more like olivine.

There are a number of possible causes of these findings. (d) *At the beginning, / Firstly*, it is (4) _____ that the sample tested is not in fact ringwoodite, but actually some other mineral, one (5) _____ from the olivine group. (e) *However, / Although* this is (6) _____ , a composition analysis is being carried out to verify the identity of the sample material. A second (7) _____ is that the multi-anvil needs to be recalibrated. This seems the most (8) _____ cause of the problem. (f) *So / Therefore*, it will be checked immediately.

b Now complete the summary by choosing the correct linking word (a–f).

14 Write a short summary describing and reporting problems you have been having with an experiment. Use the experiment you talked about in Exercises 6a and 9, or another experiment you know well. Your summary should say:

- what the problem is
- what the possible causes of the problem are

Keeping a lab notebook

15 a The abbreviations and symbols below could all be used in a scientist's lab notebook. In pairs, discuss what you think each one means.

1	△	_____	5	@	_____	9	↑	_____
2	RT	_____	6	∵	_____	10	E	_____
3	±	_____	7	∴	_____	11	w/	_____
4	w/v	_____	8	→	_____	12	~	_____

b Now match the abbreviations or symbols (1–12) to the correct meanings (a–l) below.

a about; approximately
b at
c because
d change
e energy
f increases
g leads to

h more or less (to show the deviation from the number stated)
i room temperature
j therefore
k weight per volume
l with

c In pairs, decide how you might represent each of the following in a lab notebook.

1 decreases
2 degrees Celsius
3 kelvin
4 greater than or equal to
5 positive

6 volume per volume
7 without
8 two to one ratio
9 hours
10 concentration

d What other abbreviations do you often use in your lab notebook?

e ▶ 5.6 Listen to two scientists talking about two different experimental set-ups. Complete the notes from the lab notebook with a number and/or abbreviation or symbol from Exercises 15a and 15c.

16 a In pairs, discuss the following questions.

1 How do you keep a record of your experiments?
2 Have you ever used a lab notebook software package?
3 How does the lab notebook protocol in your current lab compare to other labs you have worked in?

5 mg char into TGA pan.
Heat (1) _____ - (2) _____
- hold 30 min
= (3) _____ from last time
Heat 20 (4) _____ /min to 873 K
then (5) _____ rate -
(6) _____ K/min to 1473 K.
Gas = high purity CO_2
((7) _____ 25%) + N_2

b ► 5.7 Chuyu is asking another scientist, Mayumi, about her experiences using an electronic lab notebook. Listen and complete Chuyu's notes. Write one word in each gap.

* It's easy for people to (1) _____ information.
* You don't have to try to understand someone else's (2) _____
* You can (3) _____ your own lab book.
* All the (4) _____ you make are automatically highlighted.
* The packages can be adapted to fit your (5) _____ requirements.
* It's much (6) _____ than a paper lab book.

c In pairs, discuss the advantages and disadvantages of using an e-notebook.

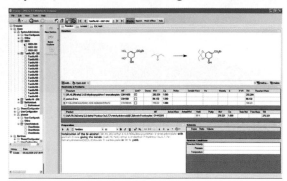

An example of a screen from an e-notebook

17 a ► 5.8 Listen to five extracts from the conversation. For each extract you hear (1–5), choose the correct description of the situation (a–e).

a describing something that people are able to do _____
b describing something that was prohibited _____
c describing something she was obliged to do _____
d explaining that it is not necessary to do something _____
e making a suggestion _____

b Look at Audioscript 5.8 on page 97 and complete the table below with the underlined phrases in the script.

	Past	Present
Ability/Possibility	could do	
Advice	should have done	
Lack of obligation	didn't have to do didn't need to do	
Obligation		must do
Prohibition		are not allowed to do can't do mustn't do

18 Work in pairs. Explain to your partner the lab book protocol you are expected to use now. Tell your partner anything that was different in a place you used to work, or the way you used a lab notebook in your past studies.

UNIT 6

Writing up research 1: materials and methods

- Describing states and processes
- Describing data: numbers / numerical values
- Writing up from lab notes

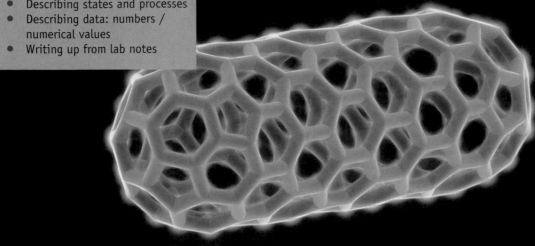

Describing states and processes

1 a Match the beginnings (1–9) to the endings (a–i) to make definitions of the words in bold.

1 A **biodegradable** substance is one which	a can be put in one place then taken away again.
2 A **nanocapsule** is a capsule which has	b into your body.
3 A **removable** object is one which	c between cells in the same organism.
4 **Endocytosis** is a process by which	d decays naturally.
5 If a cell **overexpresses** a protein, it expresses	e put inside something else.
6 If someone is given **multiple** doses of a drug, they receive	f it many times.
7 **Intercellular** communication is communication which happens	g molecules can move inside cells.
8 When a drug is **encapsulated**, it is	h a diameter smaller than 200 x 10⁻⁹ metres.
9 If you **ingest** a substance, you take it	i too much of it.

b Underline the key words in the sentence endings (a–i) which summarise the meaning of the prefixes in (1–9) (for example, bio- = naturally).

c In pairs, discuss the following questions.
   1 What is nanotechnology?
   2 What commercial applications could research in nanotechnology have?

2 a One application of nanotechnology is in pharmaceutical research. Kimiko, a PhD student, has drawn a sketch of a targeted drug delivery for the materials and methods section of her paper. What do you think is happening at each stage (a–f)?

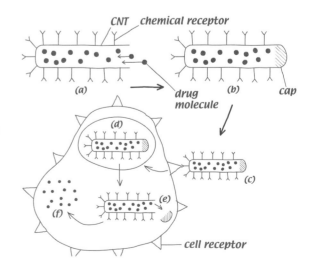

b ▶ **6.1 Kimiko asks Tom, a colleague, to look at her first draft. Listen to part of their conversation and mark the following statements true (T) or false (F).**

1 Tom asks Kimiko to make changes to her diagram. _____
2 According to Tom, some readers may only know a little about Kimiko's research subject. _____
3 Some people call nanotubes 'magic bullets' because they can be dangerous. _____
4 Kimiko's main interest is in the best method for coating a nanotube with chemical receptors. _____
5 The nanotube can be ingested in different ways. _____
6 Kimiko uses only one method to open the nanotubes after ingestion. _____

3 a ▶ **6.2 Tom asked Kimiko to explain what happens during the process. Complete the following extracts from their conversation using the words in the box. Then listen and check your answers.**

attach   by   coat   dissolves   encapsulated   in   internalised   to   with

1 To do this, first we _____ the surface of the tube _____ a chemical receptor.
2 If we want to target a tumour which overexpresses folic acid, then we _____ folate receptors _____ the surface of the nanotube.
3 And then we encapsulate the drug _____ the tube.
4 Once the drug is _____ , we use a cap to close the open end so the drug can't escape.
5 After that, the capsule is _____ _____ the cell.
6 I use biodegradable caps. The cap _____ and then …

b **The sentences below describe processes in different experiments. Match the verb in bold in each sentence (1–5) to the correct definition (a–e).**

1 A microtome was used to **slice** 4 µm sections of the paraffin-embedded tissue.	a to change from a gas to a liquid or solid state
2 As the gas cools, the water vapour **condenses** and is caught in the conical flask.	b to change the colour of something using a chemical
3 Devices in the two chimneys would **filter** out radioactive dust.	c to cut something into thin, flat pieces
4 Haemotoxylin-Eosin **stains** the cell nucleus blue and the cytoplasm pink.	d to remove or take something away
5 Plutonium 239 was **extracted** from the sample using nitric acid.	e to remove solids from liquids or gases

c **Use the glossary (pages 117–125) to check the meaning of the words in the box. Then write the verbs in the correct form to complete the sentences.**

dilute   fuse together   grind into   purify   rinse with

1 50 µl test plasma samples were _____ 1:10 with sterile water.
2 The remaining material was _____ powder for examination.
3 Steam distillation could be used to _____ the nitrobenzene because of its high boiling point.
4 The product was _____ distilled water four times using an Amicon filter.
5 When two deuterons _____ at low energy, the neutron is liberated with an energy of 2.45 MeV.

4 a Look at the extracts below from the conversation between Kimiko and Tom. Which can be used to ask politely for help and advice (A)? Which can be used to offer help and advice (O)?

1 But <u>first of all you need to</u> explain briefly what is happening.
2 <u>Do you have a moment</u>?
3 <u>I wondered if you could</u> look through it for me?
4 Sure, Kimiko. <u>What can I do for you</u>?
5 <u>Why don't you</u> talk me through it and make some notes as you go?

b Draw a diagram of a process you are working on or one you know well. Then role play a conversation in which you ask a colleague to check your diagram and your explanation of the process, using the phrases in Exercise 4a to help you.

5 a ▶ 6.3 Tom has checked Kimiko's second draft of the materials and methods section of her paper and underlined some changes he thinks she should make. Read the following extract and discuss in pairs how you could improve Kimiko's text. Then listen and make a note of the changes Tom suggests.

b Use your notes from Exercise 5a to improve Kimiko's text. Then compare your paragraph with the Answer key on page 110.

6 a We use the passive when the person or thing which performs the action is not the main point of interest in the process we are describing in the materials and methods section. Re-write sentences 1–5 using the passive voice so that they focus on the underlined word.

1 I rinsed <u>the tissue surface</u> with ice-cold isotonic saline solution.
2 After incubation at 37 °C for 60 minutes, the scientist diluted <u>the suspension</u> to 100 ml with water.
3 A mesh filters out <u>particles as small as 10 μm</u>.
4 The experiment measures <u>the audiometric thresholds at six frequencies from 250 Hz to 8 kHz</u>.
5 I used <u>densitometry</u> to analyse the autoradiograph.

b Which of the sentences (1–5) in Exercise 6a describe a process in general? Which report a particular procedure carried out in one particular experiment or set of experiments?

c Look back at the sentences in Exercises 3a–3c. Which verbs are in the passive? Which sentences could be made more formal by using the passive? Which verbs don't need to be changed into the passive?

7 Write a paragraph for the materials and methods section of a paper which describes the process you discussed in Exercise 4b. Use Tom's advice to Kimiko to write the paragraph in an appropriate style.

The magic bullet process uses carbon nanotubes to send a drug to a specific target. <u>Firstly</u>, <u>I functionalise the surface of the nanotube</u> by coating it with chemical receptors. For example, <u>for</u> target a tumour which overexpresses folic acid, folate receptors are attached to its surface. <u>Secondly</u>, <u>I encapsulated</u> the drug molecules within the nanotube. <u>Third</u>, the tube is capped and the nanotubes are ingested. <u>For example, the patient can swallow them or inhale them or have the capsules injected into them</u>. Once inside the body, the nanotube locates to the target site. <u>Fifth</u>, <u>the target cell internalises the nanotube</u> by receptor-mediated endocytosis. After that, the cap is either removed or biodegraded and the drug molecules are released into the cell.

Describing data: numbers / numerical values

8 a ▶ **6.4 You are going to hear eight short extracts in which scientists discuss their work. Read the questions below, using the glossary (pages 117–125) to check the meaning of the underlined words. Then listen to each extract and choose the correct number (a, b or c).**

1 What was the <u>dosage</u> of fluoride per kilogram of body weight?
   a 0.166   b 0.16   c 0.616
2 What was the sensitivity of the assay?
   a 0.02   b 2.0   c 0.2
3 What is the <u>output impedance</u> at the 5V end?
   a 0.02   b 0.20   c 0.92
4 What <u>amperage</u> of <u>flex</u> is used?
   a 0.6   b 6   c 6.8
5 What is the temperature below which the superconductor <u>conducts</u> electricity with no <u>resistance</u>?
   a $^9/_{10}$ b 19   c 90
6 What is the <u>enthalpy</u> change when 2 moles of water are formed at a pressure of one atmosphere and a temperature of 298 kelvin?
   a – 517.6   b – 5716   c – 571.6
7 What is the lowest frequency at which young mice squeak (make a noise) when <u>isolated</u> from their mother?
   a 450   b 45   c 405
8 What speed laser <u>pulses</u> were used?
   a 15   b 50   c – 50

b ▶ **6.5 Listen and complete the values (a–l) with the number or numbers you hear.**

a ___$/_4$ e 5 x 10——   i ___7
b ___%   f – ___5   j 17 $^5/$___
c 1___6   g ___^{6} k 0___
d 2, 9___, 7___   h 1___,893   l 5,___,019

c ▶ **6.6 In pairs, answer the following questions. Then listen and check your answers.**

1 How do we say these values?
   a ¾   b $^5/_8$ c $^4/_9$ d 10^7 e 10^{-9}
2 How do we say these symbols?
   a %   b x (in e.g. 5 x 10^9)   c –
3 What is the difference between **1.356** and **1,356**? How do we say them?

The International System of Units (SI) is the most common measurement system around the world, particularly in the fields of science, commerce and trade. It is a modern form of the metric system and as such is devised around the number 10. The system consists of 7 base units and a set of prefixes. There are a number of other common SI-derived units.

9 a Match the SI unit in column A to its abbreviation in column B and the quantity it measures in column C.

A UNIT	B ABBREVIATION	C QUANTITY
1 metre	K	temperature
2 kilogram	cd	electric current
3 second	mol	frequency
4 ampere	kg	thermodynamic temperature
5 kelvin	s	time
6 candela	m	amount of substance
7 mole	A	mass
8 hertz	Ω	length
9 joule	°C	energy
10 ohm	Hz	resistance
11 degree Celsius	J	luminous intensity

b In pairs, discuss the following questions.

1 What units of measurement do you commonly use in your everyday life?
2 What units do you use in your work?
3 Which SI prefixes do you know? How do they change the quantity?

c Look at the table below which shows the symbols for some of the SI prefixes and the factor they represent. Then complete the right-hand column using the prefixes in the box.

centi- giga- kilo- mega- micro- milli- nano- pico- tera-

	symbol	factor	prefix
1	k	10^3	_____
2	M	10^6	_____
3	G	10^9	_____
4	T	10^{12}	_____
5	c	10^{-2}	_____
6	m	10^{-3}	_____
7	μ	10^{-6}	_____
8	n	10^{-9}	_____
9	p	10^{-12}	_____

d ▶ 6.4 Listen again to the eight scientists from Exercise 8a. What unit of measurement does each one use? Write the abbreviation.

1 0.166 _____   3 0.02 _____   5 19 _____   7 45 _____
2 0.2 _____   4 6- _____   6 – 571.6 _____   8 50- _____

10 Find data for some research that you are familiar with. In pairs, take turns to discuss the key findings in the data.

Writing up from lab notes

11 **a** Kimiko has been investigating methods of encapsulating molecules in functionalised carbon nanotubes (or CNTs). Look at the extract from her lab notebook below and then match the definitions (1–8) to the words or phrases in bold (a–h) in the notebook.

1 a picture _____
2 a small piece of glass you put something on to look at it under the microscope _____
3 a small round piece of plastic, wood, glass, etc. _____
4 a small round-shaped amount of liquid _____
5 always the same _____
6 the distance between the opposite sides of something _____
7 to make something hang or float in something _____
8 an upward movement of a liquid _____

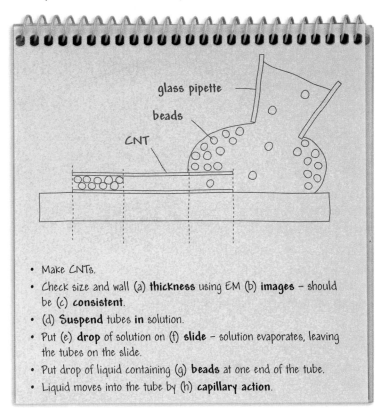

- Make CNTs.
- Check size and wall (a) **thickness** using EM (b) **images** – should be (c) **consistent**.
- (d) **Suspend** tubes in solution.
- Put (e) **drop** of solution on (f) **slide** – solution evaporates, leaving the tubes on the slide.
- Put drop of liquid containing (g) **beads** at one end of the tube.
- Liquid moves into the tube by (h) **capillary action**.

b In pairs, look at Kimiko's notes again and answer the following questions.

1 What does Kimiko use the images from the electron microscope (EM) for?
2 How does Kimiko get the CNTs onto the slide?
3 How does she get the liquid containing the beads into the tube?

12 **a** Look at another extract from Kimiko's notebook on page 52, which describes two of her experiments. Then tell a partner what the symbols and abbreviations in the box mean.

> @ ~ → D diam. EM L w/ w/v

b Look at the notes again. In pairs, what differences can you see between Kimiko's experiments of 29th October and 18th November? Can you suggest a possible way of completing the spaces (1–6)?

29th October

Tube size:
L: 10–90 μm
D: from EM – average ~ 450 nm [300–800 nm]
wall thickness: 20 nm

Tube suspension:
Float in solvent
pipette microdrop onto slides
(sticky residue remains – ?solvent blocks tube?)

Sol^n of beads:
Fluorescent polystyrene beads – D~50 nm
Float in deionised H_2O (1% w/v)
Mix w/ ethylene glycol 1:1

Dip:
Put microdrop full of beads @ end w/ plastic micropipette
Dip 6 μm tube in sol^n
→ No uptake – tubes blocked?

Next:
Suspend tubes in different solution – ethanol? propanol?

18th November

A Tube size:
L: 20–(1) ___ μm
D: from EM – average ~ 500 nm
   [300– (2)___ nm]
   (?? Deformed so real diam. smaller?)
wall thickness: (3) ___ nm

Tube suspension:
Float in (4) _____
Use dielectrophoresis to put on slides
2-propanol – dries away

B Sol^n of beads:
Fluorescent polystyrene beads – D~50 nm
Float in deionised H_2O (1% w/v)
Mix w/ ethylene glycol (5) 1:___

Dip:
Put microdrop full of beads @ end w/
(6) _____ micropipette
Dip 6 μm tube in sol^n
→ Good uptake

Next:
2 μm or 12 μm dipped – what difference?

c ▶ **6.7** Kimiko is explaining to Arnie, her PhD supervisor, what she did differently in her 18th November experiment. Listen and complete the notes (1–6) in her notebook.

13 **a** Below are two extracts from the final draft of Kimiko's materials and methods section, based on the lab notes for the 18th November experiment. Complete each extract using the words in the boxes.

A

actual   aid   and   approximately   average   due   estimated   evaporated   length   placed   ranged   suspended   to

The experiment investigated filling carbon nanotubes with a suspension containing fluorescent beads. The tubes (1) _____ in (2) _____ from 20 (3) _____ 50 μm and had an (4) _____ diameter of (5) _____ 500 nm and a wall thickness of 15 nm. The tube diameters were (6) _____ from electron microscope images and ranged between 300 (7) _____ 700 nm. The (8) _____ tube diameters may have been smaller (9) _____ to tube deformation.

The CNTs were then (10) _____ in a 2-propanol solution and (11) _____ on glass cover slips with the (12) _____ of dielectrophoresis. The 2-propanol then (13) _____ .

B

| blending | consisted | covered | filled | laden | ratio | with |

A suspension was prepared by (14) _____ ethylene glycol
(15) _____ a suspension of fluorescent polystyrene beads (1% weight/
volume) in deionised water. The bead diameters ranged from 40 to 60 nm and
the suspension (16) _____ of a 1 to 3 volume (17) _____ of
particle suspension and ethylene glycol.

A liquid microdroplet, (18) _____ with fluorescent polystyrene beads,
was placed at one end of the CNT with a glass micropipette. The drop
(19) _____ approximately 6 μm of the CNT. The suspension
(20) _____ the CNT by capillary action.

b Read through the extracts again. Which of the verbs in the box are used in:

a the passive?
b the active?

| consist cover estimate evaporate fill investigate place prepare range |
| suspend |

c Below are extracts from the materials and methods section of three different
papers and the notes on which they are based. For each extract, use the notes
to put the words from the paper in the correct order. The underlined noun
phrase at the beginning of each sentence is in the correct position.

%RBC change ~ +8.0 to -7.4

1 The change in red blood cells / approximately / from / plus / minus / 8% /
ranged / to / 7.4%.

Float cells in incubation med – into flask

2 The cells / incubation / medium / placed / and / an / were / in / then / in / a /
suspended / flask.

Stream sediment samples – soak 1:1 HCl.

3 The stream sediment samples / soaked / 1-to-1 / in / volume / a / HCl / at /
ratio / were.

14 Write a paragraph for the materials and methods section in an appropriate
style for an experiment you are working on or for an experiment you are
familiar with.

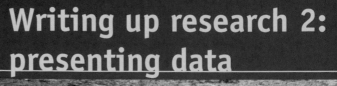

UNIT 7 — Writing up research 2: presenting data

- Analysing data (statistical analysis)
- Summarising data in visual form
- Writing captions for figures
- Describing visual data

Analysing data (statistical analysis)

1 a Some organisms have adapted to live in very extreme conditions and are known as extremophiles. Match the type of extremophile to the condition it lives in.

1 acidophile	a survives best in media with high osmotic pressures due to high sugar concentrations
2 alkaliphile	b can survive in areas with high levels of dissolved heavy metals in solution
3 cryophile	c survives best at temperatures between 60 and 80 °C
4 metalotolerant organism	d can survive ultraviolet and even nuclear radiation
5 osmophile	e survives best at pH 3 or below
6 radioresistant organism	f survives best at pH 9 or above
7 thermophile	g survives best at temperatures of 15 °C or lower

b In pairs, discuss the following questions.

1 How might research on extremophiles be useful for understanding:
   a how organisms adapt to their environment?
   b the beginning of life on Earth?
   c life on other planets in the universe?
2 What industrial and commercial applications could research on extremophiles have?

c Find a word or phrase in the definitions (a–g) in Exercise 1a with a similar meaning to the prefixes in the extremophile names (1–7). For example, *acid-* and *pH 3 or below*.

d Which suffix used in Exercise 1a (*-phile, -resistant, -tolerant*) is used to describe an organism which:

    a does not mind this environment?
    b will not be killed by this environment?
    c is attracted to and is able to exist in this environment?

Mid-Oceanic Ridge Shrimp
– *Rimicaris Exoculata*

e Match an affix (a prefix or suffix) 1–7 with its meaning a–g.

1 neutro-	a dry
2 halo-	b hate
3 hydro-	c many
4 hyper-	d more
5 poly-	e neutral
6 xero-	f salt
7 -phobe	g water

f Read the definitions of four more extremophiles (1–4). Then choose a suitable name for each extremophile using one or more affixes from Exercises 1a and 1e.

An organism that:

    1 survives best at temperatures above 80 °C. _____
    2 does not like to live in salty conditions. _____
    3 survives best at pH 7. _____
    4 survives best in very high temperatures with high metal concentrations.
       _____

2 **a** ▶ 7.1 Tiago is a marine biology student who is studying adaptations in shrimp living near hydrothermal vents. He is explaining his research to Nour, a new student in the lab. Listen to the conversation and answer the questions.

    1 What two extreme conditions have the vent shrimp adapted to?
    2 How does Tiago expect the levels of metal-binding proteins to change in the vent shrimp?
    3 How will he use the two species of Rio Formosa lagoon shrimp in his research?
    4 What other compounds is he looking at?

b Tiago is just beginning his statistical analysis. Match the words or phrases used in statistics (1–10) to the definitions (a–j).

1 Analysis of Variance (ANOVA)	a a relationship between two factors
2 coefficient	b small groups which should be representative of a whole population
3 correlation	c shows how much variation from the mean there is within the group
4 mean	d the average, found by adding all the values together and dividing by the number of values
5 p-value	e the measure of significance, which shows if it is likely that the variation in results is just chance
6 regression analysis	f the test used to compare whether the means of two groups are equal
7 samples	g the test used to produce an equation showing the relationship between two factors
8 standard deviation	h the test used to compare whether the mean values of more than two groups are all equal
9 t-test	i the things that change in an experiment
10 variables	j a mathematical value which is always written before another value it multiplies

c Tiago has written notes on how to analyse his data. Complete the notes using the words and phrases in Exercise 2b.

<u>Variables</u>
Dependent: MT levels/antioxidant levels
Independent: Different species of shrimp (2 x vent species, 2 x lagoon species)
Multiple (1) _____ from each one to accurately represent populations

<u>Statistical analysis</u>
1 Calculate (2) _____ MT level for each species
   Use (3) _____ to test whether the means of the groups are all equal
   (Could do lots of (4) _____ , but more likely to make mistakes)
2 Repeat for enzyme activity for each group
   Look for low (5) _____ to show significance (usually ≤ 0.05)
3 Look at the (6) _____ within each species – to assess variation from the mean within the group
4 Calculate the (7) _____ coefficient to see if there is a relationship between MT concentration and antioxidant enzyme levels.
   If there is a correlation, do a (8) _____ to produce an equation of the relationship
   (Use this to predict levels of MT from antioxidant enzymes or vice versa)

3 a Tiago has done some statistical analysis of his results. In pairs, look at the table below and discuss what you think the most interesting results might be.

		Hydrothermal vent species		Coastal (lagoon) species	
		Rimicaris exoculata	*Mirocaris fortunata*	*Palaemon elegans*	*Palaemonetes varians*
Metal binding protein	MT level (mg.g^{-1} w/w protein)	7.30 ± 0.66 a	1.27 ± 0.27 c	4.34 ± 0.99 b	1.65 ± 0.39 c
Antioxidant enzymes	Cytosolic SOD (U mg^{-1} protein)	2.56 ± 0.66 c	16.15 ± 5.66 a	5.14 ± 1.58 b	5.67 ± 1.73 b
	Cytosolic CAT (mmoles min^{-1} mg^{-1} protein)	0.0042 ± 0.0005 a	0.0048 ± 0.0010 a	0.0014 ± 0.0005 b	0.0020 ± 0.0005 b
	GPx (μmoles min^{-1} mg^{-1} protein)	0.010 ± 0.002 c	0.040 ± 0.010 a	0.023 ± 0.004 b	0.015 ± 0.007 bc

Values followed by the same letter are not significantly different ($p > 0.05$).

b Complete the following sentences describing Tiago's results using the words in the box.

> a significantly higher   not significantly different from   no significant differences
> approximately sixfold higher than in   the lowest   threefold higher in

1 MT levels in *Rimicaris exoculata* were _____ *Mirocaris fortunata*.
2 MT concentrations in *Palaemonetes varians* were _____ those in *M. fortunata*.
3 The hydrothermal vent shrimp *R. exoculata* exhibited _____ SOD activity.
4 _____ were found in the activity of cytosolic SOD between the two coastal shrimp species, *P. elegans* and *P. varians*.
5 The activity of cytosolic CAT was approximately _____ the two vent shrimp species compared with their coastal counterparts.
6 _____ GPx activity was observed in *M. fortunata* compared with all the other shrimp species.

c Write four more sentences comparing and contrasting the data in the box.

d Think of an experiment you have done. Explain to your partner:
- what your variables were
- how many samples you had
- what statistical analysis you needed to do and what tests you used
- what significant results you found

Summarising data in visual form

4 a In pairs, discuss the following questions.
1 Why are visuals used in scientific papers?
2 What visuals do people in your field commonly use to show data? Why?

b Match the beginnings and endings of the sentences about setting data in tables and charts.

1 Tables, graphs, etc. are necessary	a be consistent with them.
2 Visual summaries allow	b reduced in size in a paper.
3 Deciding how to present data visually makes you	c show trends; tables to show exact numbers.
4 Visuals need to be clear even when	d the reader to check the data for themselves.
5 Graphs should be used to	e think carefully about what your results mean.
6 Too much information in a visual	f to avoid filling up the text with lists of numbers.
7 Use standard symbols and	g will confuse the reader.

c Which advice in Exercise 4b do you think is the best? What other advice would you give to someone producing visuals to portray their data?

5 a Look at the visuals. Complete the labels (1–16) using the words in the box.

Tables

column	row

1 _____

2 _____

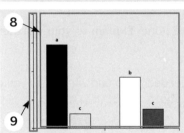

Site	Ria Formosa 37°03'N; 07°47'W	Rainbow 36°13'N, 33°54'W	Seawater
T (°C)	17.3ª	365ᶜ	–
pH	8.28ª	2.8ᶜ	7.8
H₂S (mM)	–	1.0ᶜ	~0
CO₂ (mM)	–	< 16ᶜ	–
CH₄ (mM)	–	2.2–2.5ᶜ	~0
Cd (µM)	0.9 – 4.5ª	130ᶜ	0.7
Cu (µM)	0.02 – 0.05ª	140ᶜ	0.0033
Zn (µM)	0.02 – 0.03ª	160ᶜ	0.028
Fe (µM)	8 – 52ᵇ	24000ᶜ	0.0045
Mn (µM)	2.5 – 6.3ᵇ	2250ᶜ	0.0013
Cl (mM)	–	750ᶜ	546
Co (µM)	–	13ᶜ	<2
Ag (nM)	–	47ᶜ	0.023
Ni (µM)	–	3ᶜ	<2
Si (mM)	–	6.9ᶜ	<0.2

ªInstituto Hidrográfico (1998). ᵇCaetano et al. (1997).
ᶜDouville et al. (2002).

Two-variable graphs

bar chart	histogram
line graph	line of best fit
point	scatter plot	x-axis
y-axis	

3 _____

4 _____

5 _____

6 _____

7 _____

8 _____

9 _____

10 _____

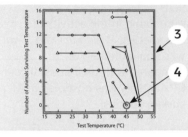

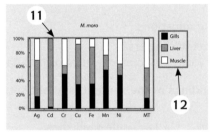

$[Cu] = 0.12 \times SW + 0.45$
$r = 0.74$

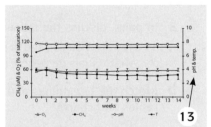

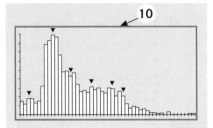

Three-variable graphs

key	label
stacked bar chart	

11 _____

12 _____

13 _____

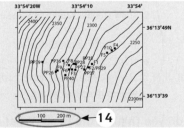

M. moro

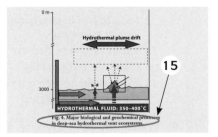

Other

caption	pie chart	scale

14 _____

15 _____

16 _____

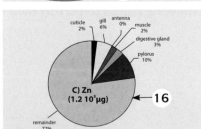

Fig. 4. Major biological and geochemical processes in deep-sea hydrothermal vent ecosystems.

b The statements below describe which type of visual is best for representing different kinds of information. Complete them using the words in the box.

> bar chart   diagram   histogram   line graph   map   pie chart   scatter plot
> stacked bar chart   table

It is best to use a:

a _____ or _____ to show a comparison between items
b _____ to show a correlation
c _____ to describe a location
d _____ or a _____ to show proportions of a whole
e _____ to describe a structure
f _____ or a _____ to show trends

6 a ▶ 7.2 Tiago has produced some visuals to depict the data from his research and is now showing them to Océane, his supervisor. Look at the bar chart in Exercise 5a and, using your own words, complete the notes on the four changes Océane suggests Tiago makes to the chart.

1 Need to label the _____
2 Units need to be _____
3 Need a key to _____
4 Use T symbols to _____

b In pairs, role play a conversation between a supervisor and a student. Student A, you are the supervisor; look at the visual on page 86 and suggest ways to improve it. Student B, you are the student; make the corrections Student A suggests. Swap roles using the visual on page 87.

Writing captions for figures

Every visual in a scientific paper should have a caption. The caption is a short text which tells the reader what the visual is showing.

7 a In pairs, discuss the following questions.

1 Should the caption appear above or below the visual it describes? Why?
2 What kind of information should the caption include?
3 What difficulties might there be when writing a caption in English?

b Read four captions (A–D) for four different figures. Then answer the questions which follow each one.

A

> Fig. 3. The relationship between the weight of shell and strontium concentration in the shell of *B. azoricus* from the Mid-Atlantic Ridge (n = 51).

1 How is the information about sample size represented?
2 Can you see a similarity in the grammatical structure of caption A and the underlined part of caption D?

B

> Table 1. Temperature, pH and concentration of chemical species in the end-member fluids of lagoon system Ria Formosa (South Portugal) and MAR vent field (Rainbow) compared with average seawater (adapted from Caetano *et al.*, 1997; Douville *et al.*, 2002).

3 Are the results in Table 1 from the author's research? How do you know?
4 Which two-word phrase explains the main purpose of the information in Table 1?

C

5   What phrase has a similar meaning to *being studied*?
6   How are the names of the organisms presented? Why?
7   What information do(es):
    a the underlined part of the caption give us?
    b the other parts of the caption give us?

D

8   What phrase has a similar meaning to *the results show*?
9   What phrase has a similar meaning to *the same for the purposes of the analysis*?
10 Can you see a difference in the grammatical structure of the underlined part and the rest of the caption?

8 a Captions often begin with a noun phrase which tells the reader what the visual shows (see captions A and B and the underlined parts of captions C and D above). Remove four words from each sentence (1–3) to make noun phrases.

1   The figure depicts the length-frequency of four samples of mussels collected at three different sites of the Lucky Strike area.
2   The figure shows the copper concentration in the soft and exoskeleton tissues of four shrimp species.
3   The table presents a comparison of the physical and chemical characteristics of the hydrothermal fluids at Menez Gwen, Lucky Strike and Rainbow (adapted from Douville *et al.*, 2002).

b Tiago's colleague, Nour, has written a caption for the following figure. Complete the caption below with the words in the box.

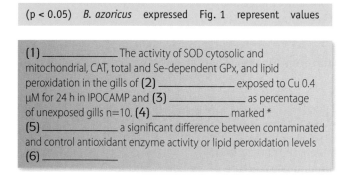

($p < 0.05$)   *B. azoricus*   expressed   Fig. 1   represent   values

(1) _____ The activity of SOD cytosolic and mitochondrial, CAT, total and Se-dependent GPx, and lipid peroxidation in the gills of (2) _____ exposed to Cu 0.4 μM for 24 h in IPOCAMP and (3) _____ as percentage of unexposed gills n=10. (4) _____ marked * (5) _____ a significant difference between contaminated and control antioxidant enzyme activity or lipid peroxidation levels (6) _____

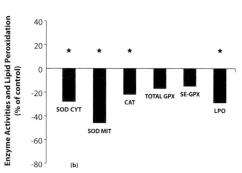

c Look at Nour's caption again. Find three parts of the text which should have brackets (parentheses) added.

d Sketch a graph for some data you are working on at the moment or that you have worked on. Write a short caption which includes all the necessary information to help explain the graph.

Describing visual data

9 ▶ **7.3 Nour is asking Océane about the best ways to describe visuals in her results. In pairs, discuss the questions (1–8) she asks Océane. Then listen and make notes on Océane's answers.**

1 Why do I need to write descriptions of my charts in the results section if they can stand alone?
2 If I have negative results, should I include those?
3 Do I need to say what the results mean here?
4 In the results section, do I need to put in every table or chart that I've produced?
5 Do I need to write about all the visuals I include in the paper?
6 What kind of things are key results?
7 When I'm describing a figure, do I need to mention every value?
8 Should I include my statistics?

10 a Look at four graphs Nour has prepared and read the two extracts (A and B) from her paper below. Which graphs (1–4) are described in extracts A and B?

A

The SOD, CAT, total and Se-dependent GPx activities and lipid peroxidation shown as a percentage of unexposed gills of *B. azoricus* are shown in Fig. 1. Cd exposure caused a significant inhibition of SOD (cytosolic and mitochondrial), CAT and total glutathione peroxidase activity (ANOVA, $p < 0.05$), while no significant change in Se-dependent glutathione peroxidase ($p > 0.05$) was seen.

B

Elevated temperature changed H_2S uptake in the three species tested differently (Fig. 3A). As temperature increased, H_2S uptake in *Alviniconcha sp.* decreased, but stayed high at the highest test temperature of 37 °C. *Alviniconcha sp.* clearly had the fastest consumption of H_2S, consistently taking up 3–4 times the quantity per unit tissue compared with the other species. For *I. nautilei*, H_2S consumption also decreased as temperature increased. *B. brevior* showed a linear pattern of increasing consumption with temperature as high as 15 °C (Regression analysis, $R^2 = 0.86$). Higher temperatures were attempted with *B. brevior*, but any exposure at those temperatures of a sufficient duration to obtain steady rates resulted in death.

b Match the underlined words or phrases in extracts A and B to a word or phrase with a similar meaning (1–15).

1 affected
2 are presented
3 expressed as a proportion of
4 fell
5 had the greatest rate of H_2S use
6 in comparison to
7 produced
8 led to
9 reduction in
10 remained at a high level
11 rose
12 showed a linear relationship of
13 up to
14 was observed
15 whereas no significant difference

11 Write a description of some visual data you are working on.

1
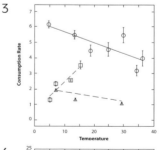

2
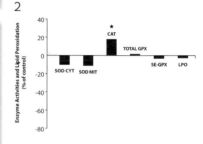

3

4
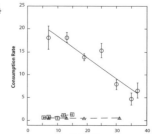

- Organising the results and discussion sections
- Preparing and writing the results section
- Preparing and writing the discussion section

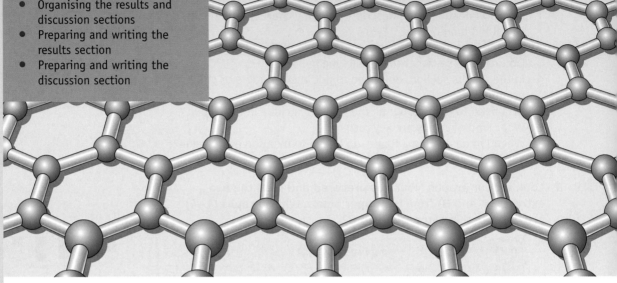

Organising the results and discussion sections

1 a In pairs, discuss the following questions.

1 How is the information in the results section of a paper different from the discussion section?
2 Why do researchers usually keep the results and discussion sections separate?
3 Why might some researchers present the results and discussion together as one section?
4 Some papers include a conclusion section. What is the difference between a discussion and a conclusion?

b Read three extracts from a research paper, ignoring the highlighted words and phrases. Then match an extract (A–C) with the part of the paper it comes from: the materials and methods section, the results section or the discussion section.

A

The majority of the activated carbons examined have surface areas ranging between 900 and 2000 m^2/g, and the ratio of micropore volume to total pore volume ranges between 0.26 and 0.65.

B

The highest storage factor attained is 89 for compacted grain-based activated carbons from rain sorghum. Therefore, sorghum-based activated carbons will be effective for natural gas storage in the fuel tanks of motor vehicles.

C

Carbonisation and activation were performed in an electrical-resistance furnace under a steady flow of gaseous N_2. The samples were contained in cylindrical baskets made from 60 mesh stainless steel gauze.

C Read the extracts again. Which of the highlighted words or phrases:

a describe(s) changes to the materials?
b describe(s) the experimental process?
c introduce(s) a significant result?
d introduce(s) the highest and lowest values that were looked at?
e introduce(s) the researcher's conclusion?
f make(s) a confident prediction?
g mean(s) the same as 'looked at'?
h mean(s) the same as 'reached successfully'?

2 a Max, a chemistry PhD student, is investigating the development of carbon-based electronics. His research focuses on the possible use of graphene in electronics. Before writing his paper, Max is reviewing some words related to his research. Complete the definitions (1–8) using the words in the box from Max's list. Then in pairs, try to guess what Max has been investigating.

> Dirac point   dope/dopant   Fermi level   impurity   layer   property of sth   sheet   ultra-thin

1 _____ (adj) very, very thin
2 _____ (n) a large thin flat (usually rectangular) piece of something
3 _____ (n) a measure of the energy of the least tightly held electrons within a solid
4 _____ (n) a quality, especially one which means that it can be used in a particular way
5 _____ (n) a substance which is mixed with another substance to change (usually lower) its quality
6 _____ (n) a thin sheet of a substance
7 _____ (n) the energy at which a solid has its lowest electron density
8 _____ (n/v) an element which is added to a substance to change its electrical properties; to add an element to a substance to change its electrical properties

b ▶ 8.1 Max is discussing his research with Florence, a new post-doctoral fellow in the lab. Listen and choose the correct word to complete the sentences.

1 Graphene is an ultra-thin layer of **boron** / **carbon**.
2 Max **adds the dopant to the structure of** / **lays the dopant onto** the graphene.
3 Max is currently using **nitrogen dioxide** / **F4-TCNQ** as the dopant.
4 Max hopes that the dopant he is currently using can reduce the **positive** / **negative** charge from the graphene layer.
5 Max also wants to know if the current dopant reacts to **air** / **water** and heat.

3 **a** Read the following extract from the draft of Max's results. Which of a–c below best summarises the main idea of Max's paragraph? Why are the other two options *not* suitable here?

    a Charge neutrality reached at 0.8 nm F4-TCNQ

    b Effect of F4-TCNQ on monolayer graphene

    c Fermi level in graphene above Dirac point

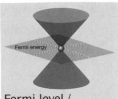

F4-TCNQ adheres to graphene sheet | Fermi level / Dirac cones

b Read the extract again more carefully and make the following corrections.

    1 Two of the sentences do not belong in the results section. Which ones are they? Where should they be in the paper?

    2 Find and correct three verbs in the wrong tense. Why are they wrong?

c In pairs, answer the following questions about the corrected paragraph in Exercise 3a.

    1 The purpose of the first sentence is to:

      a give the reader information about the structure of graphene

      b describe a key result of the experiment

      c tell the reader which table or figure has the evidence for the key result

    2 What is the purpose of the other sentences in the paragraph?

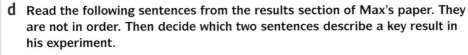

Doping with F4-TCNQ has an effect on the charge of the graphene layer. The doping level of the graphene layers was precisely monitored with ARPES measurements. For a pure monolayer of graphene, the Fermi level is located about 0.42 eV above the Dirac point (Fig. 1a). As increasing amounts of F4-TCNQ were deposited, the Fermi level moved towards the Dirac point (Figs. 1b–1d). Evidently, deposition of F4-TCNQ activated electron transfer from graphene toward the molecule thus neutralising the excess negative charge. When a 0.8 nm-thick layer of molecules is deposited, charge neutrality was reached. For a thickness of the molecular film above 0.8 nm, no additional shift of the Fermi energy is observed (Fig. 1e).

d Read the following sentences from the results section of Max's paper. They are not in order. Then decide which two sentences describe a key result in his experiment.

    a A comparison with the nonfluorinated version of the F4-TCNQ molecule, TCNQ, shows that the charge transfer increases significantly when the F4 is present.

    b As the temperature increased above 75 °C, the difference between the Dirac energy and the Fermi energy also increased.

    c Charge transfer occurs with TCNQ, but the Fermi energy always remains at least 0.25 eV above the Dirac point (Fig. 4a).

    d The difference returned to the level of a graphene layer at 230 °C.

    e The F4-TCNQ layer is sensitive to temperature.

    f The maximum shift of the band structure is obtained for a TCNQ deposition of 0.4 nm (Fig. 4d), but no additional shift is observed for higher amounts of deposited molecules.

A paragraph contains a topic sentence and one or more supporting sentences. The topic sentence contains the main idea for the paragraph. In the results section, the topic sentence of each paragraph should describe a key result and the supporting sentences should provide a summary of the relevant findings leading to the main result. The topic sentence is usually the first sentence in the paragraph.

e Look at sentences a–f in Exercise 3d again. The two sentences which described a key result are topic sentences. First, find two supporting sentences for each topic sentence. Then put all the sentences in order to make two paragraphs.

4 Think about an experiment you have been working on or that you are familiar with. What are the most significant results and the main ideas you want to discuss? Write topic sentences (only) for the results and the discussion sections of a paper and put them into a logical order.

Preparing and writing the results section

5 a ▶ 8.2 Florence is advising Max on writing up the results section of his paper. Listen and complete Max's notes with 1–3 words you hear in the conversation.

b Which part of Florence's advice do you think is most useful? Which is least useful for you? Why?

- only results - no interpretation or methodology
- highlight both my key and (1) _____ findings
- the text to follow same order as the (2) _____
- make each paragraph relate to one of my (3) _____
- include (4) _____ to my visuals in the text
- be concise (don't use (5) _____)
- use active voice and write in past tense
- can use (6) _____ to make the text clearer

c Max uses the order of his visual data to organise the text of his results section. Put the words in brackets in the correct order to complete the extracts from his results (1–4).

1 (shown / as / Fig. 1a / in), for a pure monolayer of graphene, the Fermi level is located about 0.42 eV above the Dirac point.
2 (shows / as / Fig. 1d), when a 0.8 nm-thick layer of molecules was deposited, charge neutrality was reached.
3 (be / in / Fig. 3d / observed / it / that / can) as the temperature increased above 75 °C, the difference between the Dirac energy and the Fermi energy also increased.
4 (that / Fig. 3d / shows) the difference returned to the level of a pure graphene layer at 230 °C.

6 a Max wants to compare and contrast the doping effects of TCNQ and F4-TCNQ. Read the following draft paragraph and underline the phrases he uses to describe a comparison or a contrast.

> In contrast to F4-TCNQ, the nonfluorinated version, TCNQ, showed a far less effective charge transfer, even though the fluorine atoms are not directly involved in the charge-transfer process. In the case of TCNQ, the electron affinity was 2.8 eV compared to 5.24 eV for F4-TCNQ. While charge neutrality was reached for F4-TCNQ, with TCNQ the Fermi energy remained at least 0.25 eV above the Dirac point, as shown in Fig. 4. The maximum shift of the band structure was obtained for a TCNQ coverage of 0.4 nm (see Fig. 4d), half that of F4-TCNQ, and no additional shift was observed for higher amounts of deposited molecules.

b The phrases in bold describe the results of a number of other experiments. Match the beginnings (1–8) to the endings (a–h) to complete extracts from eight different research papers.

1 At high temperature and high pressure, olivine **showed a noticeable**	a **differences were seen between** the activation efficiency of NaOH **and** KOH.
2 The carbon nanotubes **had an extremely**	b **differences** in the pH and temperature over the 3-month period.
3 For the hydroxide-to-fibre ratio of 4:1, **slight**	c **effect on** DNA synthesis and did not interact with the EGF receptor.
4 TAGH **had only a minor**	d **high** capacity.
5 The anxiety-related metabolic differences observed in urine **were significantly**	e **reduced** following 1 and 2 weeks of dark chocolate consumption.
6 **There were only marginal**	f **slower than** *C. draconoides*.
7 The robot demonstrated looping behaviour that was similar to that of the real moth and **was also highly**	g **drop in** strength.
8 When running horizontally on the high-friction surface *T. mauritanica*'s average speed **was considerably**	h **successful at** locating the odour source.

c Look at the phrases in bold in Exercise 6b and find adjectives and adverbs which express:

a a large degree

b a small degree

d Complete the paragraphs from the results section of a paper using the words and phrases in the box.

as can be seen in   considerably   contrast to   noticeably thicker   resulted in a longer while

During the rapid heating, the Ni near the Ni/SiC interface reacted with the SiC, which resulted in carbon atoms moving into the Ni. The carbon atoms then separated onto the surface of the Ni during the cooling procedure, forming graphene layers (1) _____ Fig. 1b. In (2) _____ the graphene generated using single-crystalline SiC, the graphene synthesised by this process is (3) _____ easier to remove from the SiC surface.

A slower heating rate (4) _____ process. As shown in Fig. 4, more carbon atoms were released into the Ni in a long process. Higher carbon concentration in the Ni produced a (5) _____ carbon nanofilm on the Ni surface, (6) _____ a lower carbon concentration reduced the thickness of the carbon nanofilm and formed graphene.

7 Think about an experiment you have been working on or that you are familiar with. Use the topic sentences you wrote for Exercise 4 to write at least one paragraph for the results section of a paper.

Preparing and writing the discussion section

8 **a** Max is asking Florence for advice on writing up the discussion section of his paper. Look at some of the questions Max asks Florence. Can you answer any of them?

1 Should I work through my discussion in the same order I used for the results?
2 Can I mention any new results?
3 Do I need to mention the results again?
4 Can I refer to other work that's been done in the area?
5 In terms of language, is there anything in particular I should be careful with?

b ▶ **8.3** Listen to the conversation and make notes on the answers Florence gives to Max's questions.

9 **a** Florence advises Max to use noun phrases. Noun phrases can be used to summarise a lot of information efficiently. Read a paragraph from an early draft of Max's paper. Then complete the sentence from a later draft using the words and phrases in the box.

> deposition of   electron transfer   from   movement of   towards

The Fermi level moves towards the Dirac point. When this happens, it indicates that F4-TCNQ has been deposited. When the F4-TCNQ has been deposited, the electrons are activated. When the electrons are activated, they are transferred from graphene towards the molecule.

The (1) _____ the Fermi level (2) _____ the Dirac point indicates that (3) _____ F4-TCNQ activates (4) _____ (5) _____ graphene towards the molecule.

b Complete the following sentences from three more research papers. In each space, write the noun form of the word in brackets or use *of*, *on* or *to*.

1 The _____ (able) _____ a gecko _____ walk _____ walls demonstrates that _____ (activate) _____ the adhesive system improves the gecko's movement over smooth surfaces.
2 The _____ (form) _____ a CaP layer _____ the surface allowed further crystal growth.
3 Although the species *M. fortunata* has a lower _____ (expose) to vent fluids it seems to have a higher _____ (accumulate) _____ metals in its tissues.

c Florence also advises Max to be concise. In pairs, read another extract from Max's paper on the right. Then combine the second and third sentences of the extract into one sentence in two different ways using:

a a relative pronoun (*which, that, who,* etc.)
b a VERB-*ing*

> The F4-TCNQ layer is stable in air, but appears to be temperature sensitive. At temperatures above 75 °C the energy difference increases. This increase indicates that molecular desorption occurs.

d Rewrite the following extracts from three different papers using either a relative pronoun (*which*, *that*, *who*, etc.) or a VERB-*ing*.

1 The adhesive apparatus is only activated on sloped surfaces, not on flat surfaces even when slippage occurs. This results in greatly reduced sprinting velocity on smooth, flat surfaces.

2 Consumption of dark chocolate resulted in the decrease in the stress hormone cortisol in the urine. This suggests potential benefits of dark chocolate consumption.

3 On exposure to metals, *B. azoricus* demonstrates considerable antioxidant enzymatic activity. This reflects a physiological adaptation to continuous metal exposure.

10 Look at the paragraph(s) for the results section you wrote in Exercise 7. Write a paragraph for a discussion section for those results.

11 a The discussion section of a paper often describes limitations of the current research and what experiments could be done in future. Read the following statements about Max's research and decide whether they describe a limitation (L) or an idea for future research (F).

1 ☐ The process of charge transfer has not been investigated. _____

2 ☐ Desorption might occur because of the temperature used or because of the vacuum. _____

3 ☐ Try using higher temperatures at atmospheric pressure to see what happens. _____

4 ☐ Try doping with other TCNQ-related molecules. _____

5 ☐ The graphene sample thickness is not consistent. _____

6 ☐ F4-TCNQ might be useful in silicon-based as well as graphene-based electronics. _____

7 ☐ Investigate different ways of applying the F4-TCNQ layer. _____

b ▶ 8.4 Listen to Max and his supervisor, Dan, discussing the latest draft of Max's paper. Tick the points from Exercise 11a they discuss.

12 a Based on Dan's suggestion, Max has written a paragraph for his paper on limitations and future research. Look at the underlined phrases. Which ones express limitations of the research and which suggest future research?

> The results presented here indicate that F4-TCNQ has potential as a doping agent for graphene-based electronics, but <u>further studies are needed</u>. The findings suggest that an increase in the temperature above 75 °C causes molecular desorption from the graphene surface. However, the process was carried out in a vacuum, which could be causing the desorption. <u>The results of the present study might have been different if</u> the process had been carried out at atmospheric pressure and <u>it would be beneficial to investigate this further</u>. <u>Another limitation of the study is</u> the inconsistent thickness of the graphene samples. <u>Future research should also be encouraged to examine</u> alternative methods of applying the F4-TCNQ layer. This has the potential to increase the commercial use of this doping method.

b Look at the phrases below. Which can be used to express limitations and which suggestions for future research?

1 The scope of this study did not permit us to examine …
2 Given this limitation, we do not know if/whether …
3 It is hoped that this research can serve as a basis for future studies into …
4 This is a clear limitation of the study and raises further questions related to …
5 These results are preliminary findings and suggest that further research on …

c The paragraph below describes the limitations and suggestions for future direction of a study looking at the production of graphene layers. Complete the paragraph using the words and phrases in the box.

| clear | given | hoped | indicates | permit | raises | scope | serve as |

The study (1) _____ that it is possible to produce large-area graphene films using a solid-phase-based method. It is (2) _____ that this research can (3) _____ a basis for further studies into graphene synthesis. One limitation of the present research is that the (4) _____ of the study did not (5) _____ us to investigate the differences between using 6H–SiC and 3C–SiC/Si substrates. (6) _____ this limitation, we do not know if this method is selective for the type of SiC substrate. In addition, the current study did not investigate a range of heating rates. It is possible that lower temperatures could be used if the process were lengthened. This is a (7) _____ limitation of the study and (8) _____ further research questions related to the possibility of optimising processing conditions to better control graphene production.

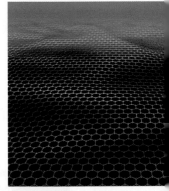
The structure of graphene

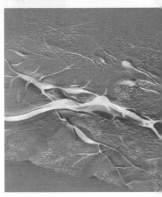
Graphene sheet

13 a Look at Max's concluding paragraph. Which sentences (1–6) explain:

a the problem?
b how other researchers approached the problem and what they found?
c the key findings of the current research?

(1) Freshly grown graphene displays an excess negative charge. (2) As presented in several other studies, approaches used to remove this charge have all displayed practical disadvantages (Riedl *et al.*, 2009; Lohmann, von Klitzing and Smet, 2009). (3) However, in a previous paper, it was shown that surface-transfer doping was a simple and reliable way to dope graphene (Chen *et al.*, 2009). (4) Recent work has suggested theoretically that F4-TCNQ could have a doping effect on graphene (Pinto *et al.*, 2009). (5) The present study has demonstrated the effect experimentally and shown that the excess negative charge in monolayer graphene can be fully compensated by functionalising its surface with F4-TCNQ. (6) In addition, we have demonstrated that the molecular layer is stable when exposed to air, preserved up to 75 °C and is totally reversible at higher temperatures.

b Underline the language used to refer to other researchers' work.

14 Write a concluding paragraph for the discussion section of the subject you wrote about for Exercises 7 and 10. Include the limitations and future direction of the research.

- Writing the introduction
- Writing the abstract
- Giving a title to your paper
- Contacting journals

Writing the introduction

1 a Mya is doing research into the panspermia hypothesis as part of a Master's degree in astrobiology. In pairs, use the diagram and the words in the box below to help you answer questions 1–3. Then compare your ideas with the Answer key on page 114.

1 What do you think the panspermia hypothesis is?
2 How credible do you think the hypothesis is?
3 What kind of evidence would support this hypothesis?

deep space   lichen   seeds of life   extremophile   meteorite   UV radiation
harsh conditions   protective layer   vehicle

b Mya has been investigating whether it is possible for bacteria and microorganisms to survive in an environment as harsh as the surface of Mars. He has been advised to organise the text of his introduction around five key questions. Match the beginnings to the endings of the questions.

What was I	approach the problem?
Why was it	expect to know after doing the research?
What was already	important?
What did I	investigating?
How did I	known about the subject of my research?

c   Read five extracts from the introduction to Mya's paper, ignoring the highlighted words for now. Which question from Exercise 1b is each extract answering? Write the questions above the extracts.

1 _____

Such an extreme environment was thought to be uninhabitable, but microbial ecology studies reported the presence of microorganisms (Amaral-Zettler *et al.*, 2002). Could the surface composition of Mars protect life against radiation?

2 _____

A number of studies have investigated different extreme Martian surface conditions on terrestrial microorganisms. Nicholson and Schuerger (2005) reported that the spores of *Bacillus subtilis* were able to survive for 19 days under Mars atmospheric pressure and composition. Saffary *et al.* (2002), however, found that survival decreased due to …

3 _____

Potential habitability in the subsurface would increase if the overlaying material did play a protective role.

4 _____

For many years now, scientists have speculated about the possibility of life on Mars (Klein *et al.*, 1976; McKay, 1997). The discovery of liquid water on Mars would increase its habitability …

5 _____

We report here on our studies of protection by Río Tinto Basin iron oxides and hydroxides on two microorganisms, *Acidithiobacillus ferrooxidans* and *Deinococcus radiodurans*, under simulated Mars surface conditions.

2   a   A well-written introduction usually presents general information about the topic first before specific information about the research. What do you think is the best order for the extracts in Exercise 1c?

   b   Answer the following questions about the extracts in Exercise 1c.
      1   Write down the highlighted words and phrases which describe:

         a   a hypothesis / hypothetical situation

         _____

         b   current research or knowledge on a particular topic

         _____

         c   general statements about past research

         _____

         d   the results or conclusions taken from specific past research

         _____

      2   What form or tense are the words and phrases in a–d above?

3 a Read an extract from the introduction of a paper about the ability of lichens and microbes to survive in deep space. Ignoring the gaps, how many of the questions in Exercise 1b can you answer?

> Recent advances in space technology (1) _____ (provide) the possibility of studying the survival of different microorganisms in the harsh environment of space (Demets *et al.*, 2005; Baglioni *et al.*, 2007). So far, lichens (2) _____ (be) the only organisms able to survive exposure to such extreme conditions (Sancho *et al.*, 2007; de los Ríos *et al.*, 2010).
>
> It is believed that, if sufficiently protected by meteorite-like material, microorganisms may also survive the journey through space. However, Brandstätter *et al.* (2008) (3) _____ (report) that microorganisms embedded in 2 cm thick rocks on the outer surface of a re-entry capsule, simulating the entry of a meteorite, (4) _____ (not survive).
>
> The aim of this work (5) _____ (be) to obtain further information on the resistance of rock-colonising microbial communities and lichens to outer space conditions, during the Biopan-6 flight of ESA on board a Russian Foton satellite.

b Complete the extract by writing the verbs in brackets in the correct tense.

4 a Read two sentences which present the same information in different ways. In pairs, try to decide what the main difference is between the two sentences. Then compare your ideas with the Answer key on page 115.

　　a　Amaral-Zettler *et al.* (2002) reported the presence of microorganisms.
　　b　Microbial ecology studies detected the presence of microorganisms (Amaral-Zettler *et al.*, 2002).

b Complete the following sentences with phrases a–d below.

　　1　We usually use an author-prominent citation when _____ and when _____ .
　　2　An information-prominent citation is usually used when _____ and when
　　　　_____ .

　　a　dealing with ideas we wish to explore in a paper
　　b　dealing with information which is not controversial
　　c　comparing ideas from a variety of sources
　　d　supporting a particular point

c A number of different reporting verbs can be used in author-prominent citations. Complete the definitions using the reporting verbs in the box.

conclude　demonstrate　discover　hypothesise　observe　prove　suggest

　　(1) _____ or (2) _____ : to use an experiment to show that
　　　　something is true
　　(3) _____ : to carefully watch the way something happens, then record it
　　(4) _____ and (5) _____ : to give a possible explanation for
　　　　something which has not been proved
　　(6) _____ : to decide something after thinking about it carefully
　　(7) _____ : to find or learn information, especially something new

5 a In pairs, take turns to ask and answer the questions in Exercise 1b about a piece of research you know well. Make a note of your answers.

b Use the notes you made in Exercise 5a to write a short introduction to your research. Remember to include author-prominent and information-prominent references in your introduction.

Writing the abstract

6 a In pairs, discuss the following questions.

1 What is the purpose of an abstract?
2 How can an abstract help a researcher choose which papers to read?
3 What information does the abstract usually include?
4 Why do some people think a good abstract is even more important in the internet age than it was before?

b An abstract usually contains one or two key sentences from each section of a paper. Read the following extracts from Mya's draft abstract. Match a section (1–4) to an extract (A–D).

1 Introduction _____   3 Results _____
2 Method _____   4 Discussion _____

A

With the aim of evaluating this possibility two microorganisms, *Acidithiobacillus ferrooxidans*, an acidophile, and *Deinococcus radiodurans*, a radiation-resistant microorganism, were exposed to simulated Mars conditions; that is, 95% CO_2, 2.7% N_2, 1.6% Ar and 0.6% H_2O with a pressure of 7 mbars. Temperature was set at 150 K and ultraviolet radiation was in the wavelength range of 200–400 nmat. Exposure was for different times under the protection of 2 and 5 mm layers of oxidised iron minerals. Survival was evaluated by growing the organisms on fresh media.

B

The resistance of organisms to extreme conditions like the conditions which exist on the surface of Mars under the protection of a thin material layer increases the possibility that life could exist on Mars.

C

Here we report that both the 2 and 5 mm thick layers provided enough protection against radiation and Mars environmental conditions for the bacteria to survive (Figs. 2 & 3).

D

Current surface conditions on Mars are extremely challenging for life. However, Nicholson and Schuerger (2005) reported that *Bacillus subtilis* was able to survive for 19 days under Mars atmospheric pressure and composition. The question is whether there are any features on Mars that could provide protection against the surface conditions. One possibility is that the surface material plays a protective role due to the fact that it is composed of iron oxides and hydroxides.

c In pairs, decide on the best order for the extracts (A–D) in the abstract. Give reasons for your answer.

7 a ▶ 9.1 Svenja, Mya's supervisor, is commenting on the draft abstract in Exercise 6b. Listen to part of the conversation and say which section (A–D) Svenja does *not* comment on.

b ▶ 9.1 **Listen again and mark the following statements true (T) or false (F).**

1 Svenja thinks the reference to Nicholson and Schuerger (2005) is useful. _____

2 Mya should remove the information on iron oxides and hydroxides. _____

3 Mya needs to include more information about the method in his abstract. _____

4 Svenja advises Mya to refer to the visuals (figures, tables etc.) in the abstract. _____

5 Overall, Svenja thinks the abstract is well written. _____

c **Look at Audioscript 9.1 on page 101. Use Svenja's advice to Mya to improve the three sections of the text of the abstract in Exercise 6b. Then compare your corrected text with the Answer key on page 115.**

8 a **Mya uses particular phrases to signal the purpose of each part of the abstract (A–D) in Exercise 6b. Underline a phrase in the extracts which Mya uses to:**

1 state the research question
2 present the hypothesis
3 introduce the method
4 introduce key results

b **The following phrases can also be used to signal the purpose of each part of an abstract. Divide the phrases (a–l) into four groups according to the functions in Exercise 8a (1–4).**

a An investigation was undertaken to explore …
b It seems likely that …
c Results show that …
d The aim of the study was to …
e The data suggest that …
f The present study investigates …
g The study provides strong evidence that …
h We demonstrate that …
i We expected that …
j We investigated a new method of VERB-*ing*
k The method involved VERB-*ing*
l … was found to …

c **The text of an abstract must be concise. Replace the underlined words in extracts 1–5 below with *that* or *those*.**

1 The hormone increased the power output of healthy volunteers by 16 per cent after four weeks of taking the drug. <u>Healthy volunteers</u> who took the drug could also exercise 50 per cent longer than control subjects.

2 We compare photographic exposure from scattered light with <u>light</u> from direct light.

3 The target yield is <u>the yield</u> which can be produced in 'perfect' conditions.

4 Structures like <u>the structures</u> described in this paper are not known in glyptodonts recorded before the Great American Biotic Interchange (GABI).

5 The lithology of failed carbonate strata differs from <u>the lithology</u> of their basal shear surfaces.

9 a Think about some research you have done recently. Write:

- one or two sentences which provide the key background to the research
- a sentence which states your research question
- a sentence which presents your hypothesis
- two or three sentences outlining the main methods used
- one or two sentences presenting the key results
- a sentence which states the key implication of your findings

b Connect these sentences to form a draft of an abstract. Use the phrases in Exercises 8a and 8b to make it clear where each section of the abstract begins. Check your work for repetition of words or ideas.

Giving a title to your paper

10 a Read the titles of six research papers. In pairs, decide which titles you think are most helpful for the reader.

1 *Staphylococcus aureus* Host Cell Invasion
2 Increase in fruit size of a spontaneous mutant of 'Gala' apple (Malus x domestica Borkh.) is facilitated by altered cell production and enhanced cell size
3 Large colonial organisms many years ago
4 Does warming alter the metabolic balance of ecosystems?
5 Cat nap: A study of Mammalian Sleep Dynamics
6 Genetic Signatures of Exceptional Longevity in Humans

b Read seven suggestions for writing the title of a research paper. Which suggestions should you use to write a good title? Which suggestions don't give good advice?

a Make it about 50 words long
b Write it as a question
c Begin with a phrase like 'A study of …' or 'An Investigation into …'
d Include a joke or play on words
e Include important key words for internet search tools
f Include information such as the species studied, the treatment used, etc.
g Present the key result

c Mya is deciding on a title for his paper and has written four alternatives. In pairs, decide which title you think is best.

1 Is there life on Mars?
2 Are there any features on Mars that could provide protection against the harsh surface conditions?
3 An investigation into whether Mars's surface material could provide protection for organisms
4 Protection for *Acidithiobacillus ferrooxidans* and *Deinococcus radiodurans* exposed to simulated Mars environmental conditions by surface material

d ▶ 9.2 Mya is discussing the choice of titles with his supervisor, Svenja. Listen to part of their conversation and answer the questions.

1 Which title (1–4 from Exercise 10c) does Svenja think is best?
2 What problem does Mya think Svenja's preferred title might have?
3 What reason does Svenja give for choosing this title?

e ▶ 9.2 Look at the three titles in Exercise 10c which Svenja thinks are unsuitable. Then listen again and make a note of:

- at least one reason Svenja gives for rejecting the three unsuitable titles.
- at least one piece of advice Svenja gives Mya about writing a title.

f Look back at your answers to Exercise 10a. Have you changed your mind about which titles are helpful to the reader? What exactly is wrong with the less effective titles? How could they be improved?

11 a Title 4 in Exercise 10c was based on the following sentence from Mya's paper. Read the sentence and then answer the questions below.

> The data suggest that *Acidithiobacillus ferrooxidans* and *Deinococcus radiodurans* are protected from exposure to simulated Mars environmental conditions by the surface material.

In Mya's title number 4:

a which phrase has been removed from the sentence?
b why has 'from' in *are protected from* in the sentence become 'for' in *protection for* in the title?
c what has 'exposure' in the sentence become in the title?

b Read the key result from four different papers. Then complete a suitable title for each paper (1–4) with a noun in each gap.

1 The findings indicate that phosphorylation can be inhibited by modifying lysine and arginine in the myosin regulatory system.
   Title: _____ of lysine and arginine in the myosin regulatory system inhibits phosphorylation

2 We demonstrate that the size distribution of organic pollutants in the air varies from season to season.
   Title: Seasonal _____ of the size distribution of organic pollutants in the air

3 The study provides strong evidence that multiple sperm factors are required to activate mouse oocytes.
   Title: _____ of mouse oocytes requires multiple sperm factors

4 We found that the multi-functional biochip made it possible to simultaneously detect the tumour suppressor FHIT gene and protein.
   Title: Simultaneous _____ of the tumour suppressor FHIT gene and protein using the multi-functional biochip

12 Look at the sentences you wrote in Exercise 9a. Use the key results to write a title for a paper on your work.

Contacting journals

13 **a** In pairs, answer the following questions.

1 Have you ever published a paper?
2 What advice would you give to someone who wanted to get an article published?

Volume 9 Issue 4 October 2010   ISSN 1473-5504

International Journal of Astrobiology

CAMBRIDGE UNIVERSITY PRESS

b Below are eight extracts from an article which gives advice on publishing your research. Match the headings (1–8) to the extracts (A–H).

1 Write your cover letter
2 Choose your journal carefully
3 Submitting your paper
4 Follow the guidelines

5 What to do if your paper is accepted
6 Reacting to a journal's response
7 What happens next
8 What to do if your paper is rejected

A _____
Talk to other researchers in your field. They will be able to suggest journals for your work and will know whether the journal has any rules that make it particularly easy.

B _____
Read the journal's instructions for authors before you submit. These are usually available on the journal's website. Look at the format of the journal's papers.

C _____
Different journals have different rules about the number of copies to submit and whether to submit electronically or in hard copy. Make sure your manuscript is submitted correctly.

D _____
Keep your cover letter short as the editor who will read it probably receives many papers.

E _____
The journal will probably contact you to say they have received your article. If you do not hear anything, send the editor a short email asking for an acknowledgement of receipt and a reference number. When your paper has been read, the editor will write to you with a decision.

F _____
The editor's letter will clearly explain how you should revise your paper before resubmitting it. If any points are not clear, write back to the editor asking for an explanation.

G _____
If the journal rejects your paper, discuss this with a colleague. It might be better to submit your paper to another journal. Do not send angry or abusive letters (!).

H _____
Ask the editor about the journal's rules about copyright and any other conditions. Finally, thank all those who have helped you, letting them know when and where the research will be published.

14 Turn to page 88. Read the letter which Mya has sent to a journal with his paper and answer the questions.

15 Using the corrected letter from exercises a and b on page 88 as a model, write a cover letter to a journal to accompany the manuscript submission of a research paper you have written (or plan to write).

- Giving a paper at a conference
- Socialising at a conference
- Presenting a poster

Giving a paper at a conference

1 a In pairs, answer the following questions.

1 Have you ever presented your research to your team or study group? How did you prepare?
2 Have you ever given a paper to a large audience at a conference?
3 Why might presenting your research at an international conference be more difficult than presenting to your team or study group?

b Look at the online poster advertising a conference and answer the following questions.

1 Who might be interested in attending this conference?
2 If a researcher applies on 7 May, could he/she give a paper at this conference?
3 If you were interested in this conference, how could you find out more?

EIMR

Coordinated by the University of Cambridge, Cambridge UK

7th annual European Malaria Conference

July 31 – August 5

Trinity College Cambridge
United Kingdom
www.eimr.org/con7

Keynote speakers
- **Zoltán Szabó**
  European Institute of Malaria Research (EIMR)
- **Miremba Kabasomi**
  Makarere University, Kampala, Uganda

Preliminary Programme
A list of other invited speakers and preliminary session topics is currently being developed by the Conference Chair and will be announced in due course. Please check back for updates.
For further information about us see www.eimr.org

ONLINE REGISTRATION ONLY
www.eimr.org/con7/registration
Registration is on a strictly first-come, first-served basis.

Application deadlines
4 April for abstract or poster presentation submissions
7 May for attendees

Registration fees
Academia – €450
Students – €350
Commercial/Industry – €650

c Complete the following words and phrases from the poster using the words in the box.

basis   course   deadline   keynote   preliminary   presentation   registration (x2)
strictly   submit   updates

1 application _____
2 on a _____ first-come, first-served _____
3 _____ speakers
4 online _____ only
5 poster _____
6 _____ programme
7 _____ fees
8 to _____ an abstract
9 in due _____
10 check back for _____

d Match the words and phrases (1–10) in Exercise 1c to the definitions (a–j).

a research summarised in a visual display _____
b an early plan for the conference (some details may change later) _____
c look for further information _____
d money you must pay to attend the conference _____
e soon _____
f the Internet must be used to send personal information for the conference _____
g the last date that personal information can be sent to the conference organisers _____
h the most important presenters at the conference _____
i the organisers will only accept applications in the order they receive them _____
j to send a written summary of your research because you want to present a paper _____

2 a The diagram below shows how the adaptive immune system responds after vaccination with an attenuated (weakened) virus. In pairs, discuss what you think the diagram shows.

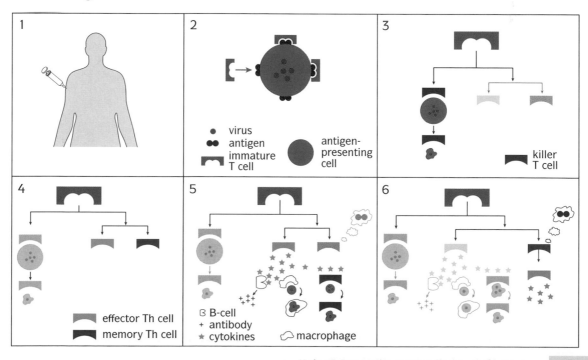

b Match the descriptions (a–f) to the correct parts of the diagram (1–6) in Exercise 2a. The first one has been done for you.

a When foreign material like bacteria or viruses is introduced into the body, the immune system acts to protect the body against the material. Vaccination makes this process happen, so the body is more ready to act if the same material is met again. _____

b Th cells cannot kill infected cells themselves. Instead, they activate and direct other immune cells. There are two groups of Th cells: effector Th cells and memory Th cells. _____

c Effector Th cells secrete cytokines. These are signalling molecules which stimulate other cells such as B cells, which produce antibodies; macrophages, which 'eat' infected cells; and Killer T cells, which attack infected cells. _____

d The memory Th cells on the other hand remember the original antigen which showed that foreign material had entered the body. If they meet this antigen again, they can immediately act like effector Th cells. In this way, vaccination can prepare the body to respond more quickly if there is re-infection with the same virus. _____

e The immature T cells then develop into either Helper T (Th) cells or Killer T cells. Killer T cells can directly attack cells which have been infected by foreign material. _____

f After vaccination, antigen-presenting cells (APC) take in the virus and then start the immune response by presenting antigens on their surface. Immature T cells bind to the antigen and recognise that it is foreign material. _____

c Measuring T-cell responses may be used to show researchers how successful a vaccine will be. In pairs, can you think of (or do you know) a method for measuring T-cell responses?

Milan is an immunology PhD student researching T-cell responses to viral-based malaria vaccines. He is presenting his research at the 7th European Malaria Conference at Trinity College Cambridge.

■ Malaria risk ■ No malaria

3 a ▶ 10.1 All the phrases in italics below are appropriate when giving a formal talk on your research. Read extracts 1–8. Then listen and underline the phrase Milan uses in each one.

1 *Good afternoon, everybody.* / *Welcome, ladies and gentlemen.*

2 *To start, thank you* / *I'd like to start by thanking you* all for coming to my talk today.

3 *I'm Milan Poborski and at present* / *My name is Milan Poborski and* I'm a PhD candidate at Northumbria University.

4 *I'm going to talk today* / *My talk today is* about my recent research investigating …

5 *I'll begin by explaining* / *To start with, I'll explain* briefly how T-cell responses …

6 *After that, I'll* / *I'll go on to* describe the alternative method I have been investigating …

7 *Finally, I will discuss* / *I'll conclude by discussing* why this method could be useful as a way …

8 *I plan to talk for about 40 minutes, leaving plenty of time for* / *I will talk for about 40 minutes and then I'll answer any* questions at the end of my talk.

b Match each pair of phrases (1–8) to their correct function (a–f) below. Note that one of the functions may be expressed with three different pairs of phrases.

    a Give instructions for asking questions. _____

    b Greet the audience. _____

    c Introduce the topic of the presentation. _____

    d Introduce yourself. _____

    e Outline the structure of the presentation. _____

    f Thank the audience for coming. _____

c Look at Audioscript 10.1 on page 101 where Milan explains the organisation of his presentation to his audience. What do you notice about the way Milan is going to organise his talk?

d Think of a piece of research you have done recently. Use the words and phrases in Exercise 3a to help you plan the introduction to a presentation about your research.

4 a ▶ **10.2 Below are five extracts from the main part of Milan's presentation. Match the beginnings (1–5) to the endings (a–e). Then listen and check your answers.**

1 A number of potential vaccine types have been developed and	a counting IFN-γ secreting cells has been the preferred method to date.
2 As I have already said,	b using flow cytometry to detect MIG secretion gives us a more accurate way of measuring immune responses.
3 As you can see from this image,	c I will be returning to those shortly.
4 Let's begin by looking at the size of the malaria problem.	d Malaria kills over one million people every year in 109 countries.
5 That's all I have to say about the vaccine itself,	e so now I'd like to move on to looking at judging the response of the immune system to the vaccine.

b The underlined phrases in Exercise 4a help speakers to organise their presentation clearly and guide listeners through the information. Write the correct underlined phrase to complete the advice below.

Use:

    a _____ : to introduce a new part of the talk

    b _____ : to conclude one part of the talk and then begin
       another

    c _____ : to refer back to an earlier part of the talk

    d _____ : to refer forward to a later part of the talk

    e _____ : to refer to a visual aid

c ▶ **10.3 Listen to five more extracts from Milan's presentation. For each extract (1–5), you will hear a new way of expressing the functions in Exercise 4b. Listen and decide which function (a–e) best describes each extract.**

d Look at Audioscript 10.3 on page 102. Find and underline the phrases which express the functions.

5 Continue the presentation plan you began in Exercise 3d. Plan how you will organise the body of your presentation. Make sentences for your presentation using the phrases in Exercises 4a–4c. Plan the visual aids you will need.

6 a ▶ **10.4 Milan has come to the end of his presentation. In pairs, look at the list (a–e) and decide on the best order for him to do these things. Then listen and check your answers.**

a ☐ let the audience know his presentation has finished
b ☐ offer the audience the chance to ask questions about his presentation
c ☐ reach a conclusion based on his research
d ☐ summarise the main points of his talk
e ☐ thank the audience for listening to him

b ▶ **10.4 Listen to the end of the presentation again and complete the following phrases using between one and three words in each space.**

1 _____ recap what I've said.
2 I therefore _____ that …
3 That _____ to the end of my talk today.
4 I would like to thank you for _____ attentive audience.
5 I would be happy to _____ you may have.

7 **In pairs, take turns to practise giving the presentation you have been preparing in this section. You may want to turn to the advice on presentations in Unit 1 Exercise 13 on page 12 to help you. Give your partner feedback on their delivery and their use of the functional phrases for organising a presentation from Exercises 3a, 4a and 6b of this unit.**

Socialising at a conference

8 a **In pairs, discuss the following questions.**

1 Have you ever been to a conference? Tell your partner about your experience.
2 Do you plan to attend any conferences in the near future?
3 What might be difficult (apart from giving a presentation) about attending a conference where the main (or only) language is English?

b **In pairs, look at the list of typical conference activities (a–h) below and then discuss the following questions.**

1 Which of these activities have you done (or might you expect to do) at conferences?
2 Which activities are easier / more difficult for you? Why?
3 Do you know any words or phrases which are appropriate for these activities?

a making arrangements for coffee, lunch or an evening out
b asking someone which talks they have been to
c asking someone for their opinion on a talk
d finding out about where someone works and what research they are doing
e asking someone if they are giving a talk
f asking someone how successful their presentation was
g introducing yourself or someone else for the first time
h networking (making useful contacts)

c ▶ 10.5 Milan is socialising at the 7th European Malaria Conference in Cambridge. Listen to extracts from eight different conversations Milan has. For each conversation, say which activity in Exercise 8b (a–h) you hear. Sometimes, more than one correct answer is possible.

Conversation 1: _____   Conversation 5: _____
Conversation 2: _____   Conversation 6: _____
Conversation 3: _____   Conversation 7: _____
Conversation 4: _____   Conversation 8: _____

9 a ▶ 10.5 Look at the sentences from the conversations in Exercise 8c. Complete the spaces with the words in the box. Then listen and check your answers.

> about   based   face   forward   giving   go   honest   how   looking   sessions   this
> turnout

Conversation 1
(1) _____ was it?
Well, to be (2) _____ it was a bit too clinical for me.

Conversation 2
And (3) _____ is Freja Pedersen.

Conversation 3
So where are you (4) _____ , Freja?
What are you (5) _____ at?

Conversation 4
So are you (6) _____ a paper here, Makareta?

Conversation 5
Well, how (7) _____ you come out with us tonight?

Conversation 6
So, how did the talk (8) _____ ?
Did you get a good (9) _____ ?

Conversation 7
So which other (10) _____ have you been to today, MIlan?

Conversation 8
It's good to finally meet you, Jacob, and put a (11) _____ to the name.
This might seem a little (12) _____ , but I wondered what opportunities there were in your lab for post-doctoral positions.

b In pairs, role play some of the conference activities (a–h) in Exercise 8b.

10 a ▶ 10.6 Listen to eight more extracts (1–8) from conversations at the conference and answer the following questions.

1   In which extract(s) is someone joining a conversation? ___ ___ ___ ___
2   In which extract(s) is someone leaving a conversation? ___ ___ ___ ___

b ▶ 10.6 Listen again. Which of the extracts do you think might be impolite or inappropriate? Why?

11 In pairs or groups of three, practise socialising at a conference. Look at the role cards on page 87 and use the language from Exercise 9a to help you.

Presenting a poster

12 **a** In pairs, answer the following questions.

1 Have you ever attended a conference poster presentation session? If so, did you speak with any presenters?
2 Have you ever prepared and presented a poster at a conference? If so, did anyone ask you questions about your research?
3 What do you think the key features of a good poster are? Make a list.

b Complete the advice below about preparing a poster using the words in the box.

> abstract   colours   columns   contact   font   heading   number   sentences
> simple   text   title   white space

General points
- Give your poster a (1) _____ which summarises the main idea.
- Keep your poster focused and (2) _____ so someone can understand the key points without any extra explanation.
- Remember that a poster is a summary of your work – so it's not usually necessary to include an (3) _____ .
- Don't forget to include your name and (4) _____ information.

The look of your poster
- Arrange information in (5) _____ .
- Use charts and diagrams as much as possible, only using (6) _____ to support your visuals.
- Give each section of your poster a clear (7) _____ in large type.
- (8) _____ each section to guide readers through your poster.
- Leave plenty of (9) _____ around each section to make them stand out more easily.

The text in your poster
- Use phrases rather than full (10) _____ .
- Try to keep phrases short.
- Choose a (11) _____ size which makes the text easy to read from a distance of 1–2 metres.
- Use different (12) _____ for different kinds of information in the poster – but remember to use them consistently.

c You are going to see two examples of conference posters and decide how well they have been designed. Do not try to read the text on the posters, but look at each one for just five seconds and think about how it looks. Then in pairs, answer questions 1–3 on your first impressions. For poster A, turn to page 89. For poster B, turn to page 90.

1 Were the posters well organised?
2 Was there space around the sections?
3 Could you see the title and section headings easily?

Which poster do you think was more successful? Why?

13 Plan the design of a poster to present a piece of your recent work. Use the advice and examples in Exercises 12b and 12c to help you.

14 a ▶ 10.7 Poster presenters should be prepared to give a short spoken summary of the main points of their research. Listen to Milan's colleague, Mosi, summarising his research and decide whether the following statements are true (T) or false (F).

1 Few researchers have studied the response of T cells to malaria vaccines. _____

2 Mosi has been investigating the response of a different kind of cell. _____
3 Mosi has used both mouse and rat models in his research. _____
4 Vaccination changed the numbers of one type of cell. _____
5 Mosi concludes that T cells are a good marker of immune system response to vaccines. _____

b Look at Audioscript 10.7 on page 102. Match the underlined phrases to functions 1–5 below. One of the functions is expressed with two phrases.

1 drawing conclusions from the research _____
2 explaining how the present research is different _____
3 explaining previous research in the area _____
4 highlighting the key results _____
5 introducing the method _____

15 a ▶ 10.8 Poster presenters should be prepared to answer questions from conference participants about their research. Listen to the answers (A–C) that Mosi gives to three questions from a conference participant. Write A, B or C next to the correct question.

- Could you just clarify how the NK cells could be affecting T-cell responses? _____

- Can you tell me what method you used to measure the T-cell and the NK-cell responses? _____
- I can't remember what the difference is between $CD56^{bright}$ and $CD56^{dim}$ NK cells. Can you remind me? _____

b At the end of each answer, Mosi asks a question or makes an offer to the participant. Put the words in brackets into the correct order.

1 (about / what / that / you / to / know / is / wanted) them?

_____

2 (more / want / about / to / know / you / if) the specifics of the protocol or the reagents I used, (an / email / me / just / send). The address is here, on this handout and on my card.

_____

3 (your / answer / does / that) question?

_____

16 a Using the poster plan you created in Exercise 13, plan a two-minute explanation of your research.

b Present your explanation to a partner along with your poster plan. When you are listening, try to ask one or two questions at the end. When you are presenting, answer your partner's questions. Be sure to check that you have really answered their question at the end.

ADDITIONAL MATERIAL

Unit 1

9 a

CURRICULUM VITAE
Carlos Manuel Alvarez

PERSONAL INFORMATION

Address:	3 Woodstock Drive	Email:	cma007@qmail.com
	London	Home Phone:	020 8083 8833
	SE17 1WY	Mobile:	07979 122177
		Nationality:	Spanish

EDUCATION

1994–1999	Instituto El Burgo De Las Rozas, Madrid
1999–2001	Collegio Madrid
	Bachillerato
2001–2006	University of Barcelona, Spain
	Licenciatura en Ciencas (Equivalent to BSc + MSc) Grade: 8.26/10
	Courses studied included: Wetland Plant Ecology; Plant Population Ecology, Plant Diversity
2003–2004	Exchange student to Bristol University, UK
2005–2006	Final year research project: *'Developing botanical indicators for integrated coastal habitat management'*
2008–Present	University of Seville
	PhD candidate

Unit 7

6 b A

Site	Menez Gwen		Rainbow
T	271–284	185–324	365
pH	4.5	3.4–5.0	2.8
H_2S	1.5	0.6–3.4	1.0
CO_2	17–20	8.9–28	<16
CH_2	1.35–2.63	0.5–0.97	2.2–2.5
Cl	380–400	413–554	750
Si	8.2–11.2	8.2–16	6.9
Mg	0	0	0
Sr	100	80–130	200
Fe	<2–18	70–920	24000
Mn	59–68	77–450	2250
Cu	<2	<2–30	140
Zn	<2	<2–40	160
Cd	<9–12	18–79	130

Unit 7

6 b B

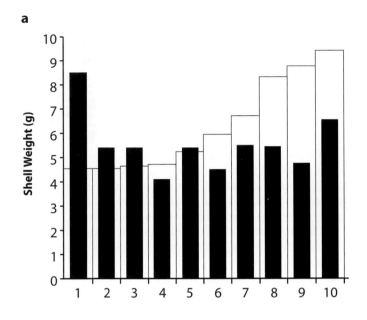

Unit 10

11

Student A
Introduce yourself.
Find out about where B works and what their research interest is.
Find out if C is presenting at the conference.
Answer any questions you are asked.

Student B
Introduce yourself.
Find out if A is presenting at the conference.
Find out if C went to the opening talk and
if so, what they thought of it.
Answer any questions you are asked.

Student C
Introduce yourself.
You gave your paper today. Explain how it went.
Find out what good talks A has been to.
Invite A and B to meet you later.
Answer any questions you are asked.

Dear Dr Tua,

Please find (1) <u>with this letter</u> a (2) <u>draft paper called</u>
'Protection for *Acidithiobacillus ferrooxidans* and
Deinococcus radiodurans exposed to simulated Mars
environmental conditions by surface material' which
I am (3) <u>sending only to you at</u> the *International Journal
of Astrobiology* for publication as a full-length article.
The paper demonstrates that a 2 mm thick layer of oxidised iron minerals
provides enough protection against radiation and Mars environmental conditions
for the *Acidithiobacillus ferrooxidans* and *Deinococcus radiodurans* to survive.
It (4) <u>gives more information on the work</u> by Ungwe, published in Issue 17 of
the journal. This finding increases the possibility that life could perhaps exist on
Mars. This paper should (5) <u>be interesting for people in</u> astrobiology, planetary
science and extremophile research.
(6) <u>A person who could check the paper is</u> Tom Ungwe (tungwe@umal.ac.uk)
since, as mentioned, this work further develops his recently published findings
on *Acidithiobacillus'* polyextremophile nature. (7) <u>I don't want</u> Mia Brown of
South Lakes University <u>to review the work.</u>
Thank you for (8) <u>looking at my article</u>. Please (9) <u>write about this article</u> to me
at the University of the North or by email (mmya@UOTN.ac.uk).
Yours sincerely,

Mya

Mya Mya (Mr)
Attachments:
Manuscript – 'Protection for *Acidithiobacillus ferrooxidans* and *Deinococcus
radiodurans* exposed to simulated Mars environmental conditions by surface
material'
Completed Copyright Transfer Form

a Has the letter been written in an appropriate style?

b Replace the underlined words and phrases (1–9) in Mya's letter with the
more suitable phrases in the box.

> address all correspondence concerning this manuscript   enclosed   extends the research
> I would prefer that … not be approached to referee this research.
> knowledgeable referees for this paper might include
> manuscript entitled   submitting for the exclusive consideration of
> therefore be of interest to those in the field of   your consideration of my work

ERP measures of material specificity for crossmodal relational memory

Greg Savage[1]   Blake Johnson[1]   Megan Willis[1]   Stuart Lee[2]   Genevieve McArthur[1]

[1]Macquarie Centre for Cognitive Science (MACCS), Macquarie University
[2]School of Psychology, Psychiatry & Psychological Medicine, Monash University

MACQUARIE UNIVERSITY | MACQUARIE CENTRE FOR COGNITIVE SCIENCE

The issue

Unilateral brain disorders can show *material specificity* on memory testing:

- verbally-mediated testing reliably assesses left hemisphere (LH) memory problems
- "nonverbal" testing assesses right hemisphere (RH) memory problems
- BUT : nonverbal findings are not reliable, posing problems for neuropsychologists, neurosurgeons, and ultimately, patients

Specific problems

Conceptually :
- what counts as *nonverbal* test material?
- designs, faces most commonly used

Methodologically:
- nonverbal tests can be *verbalised*
- verbal/nonverbal tests are not *matched*
- known vs novel content
- auditory vs visual mode of presentation
- recall vs recognition mode of response

Specific solutions?

Conceptually : appeal to cognitive models
- RH: spatial location, melodic contour
- LH: orthographic/phonological processing

Methodologically:
- use nonverbal materials which *can't be verbalised*; use verbal materials which aren't imageable
- match verbal/nonverbal subtests
- make all items novel
- use *both* visual and auditory modes
- use Yes/No recognition responses only

Methods

24 healthy Ss; 6 subtests: verbal/nonverbal versions of visual, auditory, and crossmodal pairings

displayed nonwords (vis NWs)   spoken nonwords (aud NWs)   crossmodal NW pairs
plentron ⇨ /meidrænt/   plentron + /meidrænt/

displayed dot patterns (dots)   played melodies (tunes)   crossmodal dots-tune pairs
(synthesised piano)   (synthesised piano)

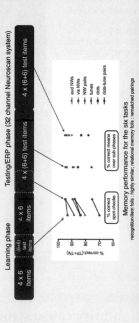

Learning phase   Testing/ERP phase (32 channel Neuroscan system)

Memory performance for the six tasks
recognition/item foils : highly similar; relational memory foils : rematched pairings

Temporal analyses

N1 responses : verbal-nonverbal differences only at bilateral parietal sites (P7, P8)
Material specificity : LH responses larger for nonwords, RH responses larger for dots

Spectral analyses

Gamma (35-45 Hz) activation for crossmodal pairings showed *material specificity* : LH activation larger for nonword-nonword pairs, RH responses larger (trend) for dots-tune pairs

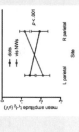

Verbal nonword-nonword pairs

Nonverbal dots-tune pairs

Conclusions

- ERPs showed material specificity in recognition memory for both verbal and nonverbal materials, matched for novelty, presentation modality, and testing mode
- Singleton and relational paradigms both show material specificity
- Clinical memory tests should contain well-matched verbal and nonverbal subtests; nonverbal subtests could usefully incorporate spatial patterns and melodic stimuli

Insect aquaplaning:

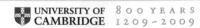

Wetness-based activation of traps in *Nepenthes* pitcher plants

Ulrike Bauer and Walter Federle

Pitcher plants use various structures to capture prey

Nepenthes pitchers are highly specialised leaves to attract, capture, retain and digest arthropod prey. Specialised trapping structures include a viscoelastic digestive fluid, slippery wax crystals and downward-pointing cells on the inner pitcher wall, and the pitcher rim (peristome) which causes insects to 'aquaplane' when it is wet. We investigated the relevance of individual structures in the field by comparing two forms of *N. rafflesiana* with different combinations of pitcher traits.

Different combinations of trapping structures in 2 forms of *N. rafflesiana*

typical form   elongate form

	typical form	elongate form
slippery peristome	✓	✓
wax crystals	✗	✓
downward-pointing cells	✓	✓
viscoelastic fluid	✓	✗

Peristome and wax crystals are relevant for natural prey capture

The test:
'Knock-out' manipulations of individual structures:
- **surfaces** coated with transparent, odourless silicon polymer
- **fluid** replaced with water

Observation of natural prey capture

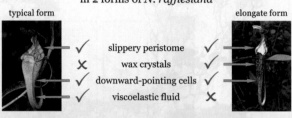

The answer:
Only **wax crystals** and the **peristome** are relevant

But:
Many species do not have wax crystals!

And:
The peristome is only slippery when it is wet!

Rain and air humidity cause strong variations of capture efficiency

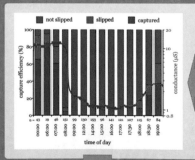

The test:
Measurement of...
- **peristome wetness** (as electrical conductance)
- **capture efficiency** (running tests with ants)
- **meteorological data** (rainfall, temperature, air humidity)

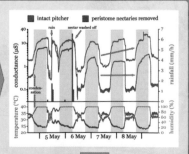

Research supported by:

Trinity College Cambridge
Zoology UNIVERSITY OF CAMBRIDGE

Capture efficiency and peristome wetness vary synchronously

Wetting is caused by rain, condensation and nectar

1.1

Susana: … and have you thought about what you'll do once the PhD is finished?

Eriko: I don't think of much else! It's actually rather scary. I know I don't want to abandon science and become an accountant, but beyond that …

Susana: Well, let's start with a simple choice. Academia or industry?

Eriko: Oh, easy – academia. I've really enjoyed the teaching I've done, so I don't want to give that up.

Susana: But in industry you could supervise more junior researchers. You wouldn't have to give up teaching.

Eriko: No, but it's different. I find it really interesting to explain quite complex topics. Supervising people would be more practical. I really love communicating the theory side of things.

Susana: Well, yes … but I don't think working in industry rules that out. It would just be different. You would also be out in the field more. Someone would pay you to go to real disasters to try the robots out.

Eriko: Hm. That's true. But I'm not so interested in doing that. As long as I have time to do work on developing the robots in the lab, that's fine for me. I do really want to teach though. I actually quite enjoy preparing lectures and thinking of creative ways to get the information across.

Susana: Really? OK, so assuming you go for academia …

Eriko: I'd like to get a post-doc position first.

Susana: OK. And any idea who you'd like to work with? Or where you're looking at?

Eriko: Not really … I'm going to leave here, though.

Susana: Oh? You don't like London? The university?

Eriko: No, I do … but I did my Master's here, part-time, while I was working as a research assistant in the lab. And then I transferred to the PhD while still working. So, basically I've done everything here, and I really think I should change, move on.

Susana: You're quite right. Going somewhere else is a very good idea – I hadn't realised you'd been here for so many years.

Eriko: I came on a student visa nine years ago and never went back. Anyway, applications for a couple of interesing post-docs at Cambridge close early next month.

Susana: They get earlier every year! I'll look over them before you send them off, if you like.

Eriko: That'd be great. I doubt they'll want me, but I might as well give it a go. And then I'm meeting a couple of people from the University of Glasgow at the conference next month. Just for a chat.

Susana: Well, it sounds like you're doing the right things. So then you'd be looking at a full-time position in higher education after that?

Eriko: Yes.

Susana: And all the paperwork doesn't put you off?

Eriko: Well. I don't actually mind it that much. So no, it doesn't bother me.

Susana: And the money? You're not tempted by the salaries in industry?

Eriko: Not at all. Well, maybe a bit. But there are more important things than money. I know I'm not going to get rich this way. But industry work? I really don't think it's for me.

Susana: But it's good to know it's there as a possibility.

Eriko: That's true – if things don't work out …

1.2

1 And then I'm meeting a couple of people from the University of Glasgow at the conference next month.
2 But I did my Master's here, part-time, while I was working as a research assistant in the lab.
3 But I'm not so interested in doing that.
4 But in industry you could supervise more junior researchers.
5 I find it really interesting to explain quite complex topics.
6 I'm going to leave here, though.
7 So, basically I've done everything here.
8 You would also be out in the field more.

1.3

Eriko: So if I use the research experience heading, do I include presentations, publications, grants, awards, skills and everything all in there? I mean, won't the section be too long?

Susana: You're absolutely right … it would be too long. I think this is one of the big differences between a CV in English and the résumés most of us learned to write. In a CV you can use a lot of different headings for the various sections. So you can have a research experience heading where you list your research positions, but then separate headings for the other details, the publications and so on.

Eriko: OK, so let me just check I've got this right. I should start with a personal information heading, and then next is education. Could I just ask one thing about that?

Susana: Sure.

Eriko: In the education section, how far back should I start? I mean, which school should be first? Not elementary school, I assume.

Susana: Ah, well, another thing here. In CVs, they always write the most recent thing first. So in education, your PhD comes first, just after the title.

Eriko: So … what … in publications, the paper I published last is written first, right?

Susana: Right.

Eriko: Hmm, OK …

Susana: … and as to which education to mention, I'd start with high school at the earliest, nothing before that.

Eriko: OK, so start with Osaka University.

Susana: Exactly.

Eriko: And after the education section, research experience and then technical skills, followed by publications …

Susana: No, no, no – put your teaching experience next, after technical skills, because you'll hopefully be doing some teaching.

Eriko: OK, so research experience, technical skills, teaching experience, publications, OK fine, and *then* grants and awards and finally presentations. Is that the lot?

Susana: Yeah, that should be good. So you'll be OK now?

1.4

Eriko: OK. Are you ready?

Carlos: Yes, yes. I am ready.

Eriko: You sure? OK? Just stop me if there's a problem.

Carlos: I will, don't worry! OK, good, go, go!

Eriko: OK then … here it is … Hello. My name is Eriko Oshima and I'm currently a PhD candidate at Imperial College London. My research—

Carlos: Oh! Eriko … too fast, I think, slow down a little.

Eriko: OK, yes … Hello. My name is Eriko Oshima and I'm currently a PhD candidate at Imperial College London. My research focuses on developing odour-sensing robots. This is useful because humans have a poor sense of smell, and so we have to rely on other methods to …

1.5

Eriko: So how was it, Carlos?

Carlos: Well, you remembered everything, and you spoke more clearly, and not too fast, but …

Eriko: But what?

Carlos: Well, one thing is you sound very bored. Your voice is always at the same level.

Eriko: So … ?

Carlos: Well, if you listen to English-speaking people, they stress the important words. They make them louder and stronger.

Eriko: And their voice goes up and down more?

Carlos: Right. So try to work out which your important words are and stress them. And another thing connected to this is that you don't pause enough.

Eriko: I don't?

Carlos: Well, sometimes you do, but not always at the right time.

Eriko: So I guess I should plan when to pause too.

Carlos: That's a good idea. And there were some words you had problems with.

Eriko: Yes, it's really hard for me to say 'detect part–' … 'detect particular' … argh!

Carlos: So I guess you just need to practise those problem words or groups again and again.

Eriko: Argh! It's so hard!

Carlos: Why don't you ask an English speaker to record it for you? Then you can listen and try to copy them.

Eriko: That's a good idea – maybe I can ask Doug …

▬ 1.6

Eriko: Hello. My name is Eriko Oshlma and I'm currently a PhD candidate at Imperial College London. My research focuses on developing odour-sensing robots. This is useful because humans have a poor sense of smell, and so we have to rely on other methods to detect particular odours. For example, we use trained sniffer dogs to locate people trapped in buildings, chemical leaks or illegal drugs. However, there are a number of problems with using dogs. First they cannot communicate exactly what they have detected. But a robot could. Secondly, it is difficult to tell if an animal's sense of smell is in some way impaired. But a malfunctioning robot would be easily spotted. Third, animals require extensive training with …

▬ 1.7

1 Hello. My name is … and I'm currently …
2 My research focuses on …
3 This is useful because …
4 For example, …
5 However, there are a number of problems with …

▬ 2.1

Ryuchi: Martina? Before I start the review I just want to check a couple of things.

Martina: Uh-huh …

Ryuchi: So first, how long should my review be?

Martina: So, for this one, you should be able to do it in a couple of paragraphs. In the first one, start with a brief summary of the research and then go on to a second one which gives your opinion.

Ryuchi: And usually I just read the abstract, to find out about the research … so, can I write a critical review if I've only read the abstract?

Martina: Hm, not really. I mean, in terms of the summary, you could get pretty much everything from the abstract, but it really won't help you to do a good critical review. You need to have read and understood the whole paper properly before you can judge how good it is.

Ryuchi: Hmm … I guess that's true. So in that case, how should I approach the reading? What should I read first?

Martina: Well, of course you should read the abstract first to get a very general idea … then focus on highlighting the key information in the Introduction, Methods, Results, and Discussion. I'd draw up a table to fill in the key points.

Ryuchi: Something like this?

Martina: Yeah, that looks great.

Ryuchi: Is it a good idea to think of questions I want answered? Like I've done here?

Martina: Yes, it's really good to have those key questions written down. They'll help to keep you focused while you're reading and note-taking.

Ryuchi: Yeah, someone else suggested I do that. And you mentioned note-taking. Do I need to take notes or can I just highlight the relevant bits of the text?

Martina: Well, you could simply highlight, but it's really important when you write the summary that it's in your own words. So if you make notes in your own words, that will help you later.

Ryuchi: Good point. And I've added this column to make notes on what I think is good and bad as I go along. To do the critique later.

Martina: Excellent idea. So why don't we …

▬ 2.2

Ryuchi: … So I read the paper, by Martin *et al.*, and, well, I don't think it's very credible.

Martina: OK, so can you talk me through it?

Ryuchi: OK, so, method. They studied 30 young healthy adults, and gave them 40 grammes of dark chocolate a day for 14 days.

Martina: Hmm, and do you think that's an effective sample?

Ryuchi: No, it's too small. And I also think the trial period is too short … not long enough to get any real results.

Martina: OK, good, carry on.

Ryuchi: Another thing is that before the trial started they assessed their anxiety levels with a questionnaire.

Martina: Uh-huh.

Ryuchi: And then they divided them into high and low anxiety groups.

Martina: Uh-huh. And why might that be a problem?

Ryuchi: Well, it's a problem because it reduces sample size even more, right?

Martina: Yes, absolutely right.

Ryuchi: Then on days 1, 8 and 15 they took blood and urine samples to look for changes in cortisol and catecholamines in the urine and for differences in energy metabolism and gut microbial activities.

Martina: So what you're saying is that they didn't actually look at changes in stress levels or reported anxiety?

Ryuchi: No. They didn't. And another thing I thought was strange was that there was no control group.

Martina: There was no control group?

Ryuchi: No, so they were comparing high and low anxiety groups only.

Martina: So thinking about the discussion section – what does that tell us? Do you think they can prove it was the chocolate that caused the changes?

Ryuchi: Mmm. No, I guess they can't, really.

Martina: Good. So tell me what you think they would need to do to make this a valid study?

Ryuchi: OK, so first, they need a larger number of people with the same anxiety levels. And then, after that, they should give them either dark chocolate or a … a … I forgot the word. What do you call it when you tell some of the participants that you are giving them chocolate, but really, you are giving them something different?

Martina: A placebo?

Ryuchi: Ah yes, placebo. They should give them either dark chocolate or a placebo.

Martina: Yes, they should. Good.

Ryuchi: Over the long term they should look at stress levels, reported anxiety and health as well as the metabolic changes.

Martina: Good.

Ryuchi: Oh, and the researchers should *not* know which group each subject is in. So it's a blind trial.

Martina: Yes, I agree completely. So the next thing …

▬ 2.3

Binh: … Yes, I have that. OK, so recipient researcher? I assume that is you, rather than me.

Alina: Yes, so Dr Alina Piotrowska is fine.

Binh: And is the address OK too?

Alina: Yes, that's fine. So, the material is coming from the Liverpool Tissue Bank, good, and you're asking for breast tissue microarrays, that's fine as well, and paraffin wax embedded, *dobrze*, very good.

Binh: OK, so the rest of the form.

Alina: Well, this work is not through any industrial partners.

Binh: So that's a 'no' here? In the part about existing arrangements?

Alina: That's right … and it doesn't have commercial potential, or you're not going to make money from it at least. They ask about that again, just here, so put no in now.

Binh: Right. Next, so, is this material hazardous? No.

Alina: Yes, yes, it is. Any human tissue is classed as hazardous.

Binh: Even when it's fixed?

Alina: Even when it's fixed.

Binh: So then does it require BioSafety Committee Approval?

Alina: Yes. But not Ethics Committee. That's only for live subjects.

Binh: Right. So yes for biosafety and no for ethics.

Alina: And we already have the BioSafety Approval … so yes for that question.

Binh: Oh … I don't even know what the next question means.

Alina: Oh, right … well, one of the reasons we fill in these MTAs is so it's clear who the material and the findings belong to. In some cases, even though you do the work, as the tissue is from the Liverpool bank, they still have certain rights regarding the data.

Binh: Ah, yes, I meant to ask about that. The forms for the provider say that I have to give them my raw data when I've finished the project. Is that normal?

Alina: Yes – so the IP will be held by both us and them together.

Binh: IP?

Alina: Intellectual Property. In this case, who owns the findings in other words.

Binh: OK.

Alina: And because you are doing the work but the tissue bank wants copies of your data, we have to arrange to have a talk about what that means for you. That's why they want to know if university students are involved … so, you can say yes here to the last question.

Binh: OK, thank you so much. Erm, Part B …

▮▮ 3.1

Rayna: … So, as I said in my email, I think we could create a material which mimics the surface of the beetle's wings and so could be used to harvest water from fog.

Bryn: Yes, that might be possible, but I don't believe it would be any better than the lotus-inspired surfaces Meera and Zein are working on. In fact, what you are proposing seems to double the work – you'd need a hydrophobic and a hydrophilic surface.

Rayna: That's true, but it seems to me that this would be more efficient.

Bryn: In what way?

Rayna: OK, as far as I'm aware, the lotus-inspired materials collect actual droplets of water, drops of rain. But this beetle seems to be able to collect water just from fog, not raindrops, so you wouldn't need actual rainfall.

Bryn: Yes, I can see that …

Rayna: But to mimic its surface—

Bryn: Sorry, before you go any further, what use do you see for this material?

Rayna: Oh, I think it could be useful in, say, refugee camps to collect drinking water or …

Bryn: But I can't see how it would be better than the fog-catching nets which already exist.

Rayna: Oh, well, I think nets must be less efficient because of the holes in them. Surely some of the potentially useful fog blows straight through them?

Bryn: Hmm, I suppose so.

Rayna: So a lot of water is lost. And as well as creating a material to collect water for refugees, another use might be in cooling towers, to recycle the water.

Bryn: Aha, now that sounds like a profitable use. Yes, I can see that.

Rayna: So do you have any idea how to make this material? I guess we could use microcontact printing.

Bryn: We could, but I feel there must be a simpler way than that …

▮▮ 3.2

Rayna: I think we could create a material which could be used to harvest water from fog.

Bryn: Yes, that might be possible, but I don't believe it would be any better than the lotus-inspired surfaces Meera and Zein are working on.

Rayna: That's true, but it seems to me that this would be more efficient.

▮▮ 3.3

1 Sahal

Before I went to the meeting, I thought my listening and speaking skills were quite good, but when I got there, I realised how hard it was to listen to so many people. When you're talking one-on-one, it's easy to follow and join in the conversation. But at the meeting, the topic seemed to change before I'd had time to understand what had been said. I didn't manage to say anything at all and left totally confused.

2 Hitomi

In Japan, we let one person finish what they're saying before we start to speak. It's polite. At the first meeting I went to, everybody seemed to talk at the same time. People weren't even interrupting politely. They just talked over the top of each other. It got louder and louder. I wanted to join in, but there was no chance for me to say anything. At the next meeting, I was more confident, but it was still hard for me to speak when someone else was already talking.

3 Sam

Most meetings in my department are quite short, only about 30 to 45 minutes long, but when I first started attending, they seemed to go on for ever. I could understand for about the first 15 minutes, but after that I couldn't keep concentrating and so I would miss important information. The worst time was when someone asked my opinion and I had no idea what they'd been talking about.

4 Radek

The biggest problem I have at meetings is knowing how formal or informal my language should be. I'm not really sure which phrases are slang and things, you know. It's a real problem when I want to disagree with someone, without being rude, or when I want to ask what someone means or stuff like that.

▮▮ 3.4

Sarah … so the gecko's ability to stick is basically, it's all to do with the forces between the setae and the surface.

Ali: Sorry, Sarah. Could I just ask what kind of forces?

Sarah: Well, for a while, people thought it could be capillary, but now it seems it's mainly Van der Waals forces, with just a little bit of capillary force.

Ali: Oh, OK.

Sarah: As the gecko moves, the setae are angled so that the spatulae sit flat against the surface. It seems the setae are pushed against the surface and then slid back slightly to get maximum sticking force.

Ali: Erm, sorry. Can I just check I understood? So what you're saying is that the ability of the gecko to stick is not just because of these spatulae, but because of the whole locomotor system.

Sarah: That's exactly right.

Deepak: So you're clear on the adhesion mechanism now, Ali?

Ali: Yes, I think so. Sorry, Deepak.

Deepak: That's OK. Right, so as I was saying, what I've been looking at is the effect of the geometric asymmetry of setae on their mechanical response.

Ali: Sorry, could you quickly explain that? I'm not quite sure what you mean.

Deepak: Sure. Erm … so, at first, most of our studies of setal deformations used a single cylindrical pillar to simulate a seta. But then, of course we know from images that they're actually curved.

Ali: And don't stick straight out.

Deepak: Of course. We did look at forces with the pillar at an angle too, not just sticking out perpendicular to the surface. But what I mean is it was always straight, not curved.

Ali: OK, sorry, you were saying.

Deepak: Anyway, because we know now that they are curved, we've been comparing a curved model with the straight pillars. So, what we've found is—

Ali: Erm, could I jump in and ask a question? Why are you focusing on forces in one setae … one seta on its own?

3.5

Deepak: So as Sarah was just saying before Ali interjected, the bottom of the gecko's foot is covered in ridges, which themselves are covered in many, many setae. The setae have flattened ends, spatulae, which when aligned correctly with the surface, allow the gecko to stick, via the Van der Waals forces we were talking about.

Ali: No, I've got that, but what I mean is, why just focus on one set–seta? It seems to me that you need more than that …

Deepak: Of course. Well, measuring the forces of one seta, whether the adhesive or shear forces … those are the forces …

Ali: No, I know what they are …

Deepak: OK, well, our analysis of the forces allows us to show the differences between asymmetric, curved pillars and straight, to show why the curved ones are more suitable for gecko adhesion. Obviously we can then scale that up to the whole animal.

3.6

Ali: Sorry, I don't think I expressed myself clearly. It seems to me that something is missing here. Surely it's important that the setae are part of a gecko.

Sarah: Deepak, I think what Ali is saying is that for the gecko to stick to the ceiling, the whole gecko has to be involved. It doesn't stick simply because its setae are curved, or because the spatulae are aligned in a particular direction. Am I right, Ali?

Ali: Yes, thanks, Sarah. Yes, what I wanted to say is that, from what I understand, the whole system needs to be working together for the gecko to stick.

Deepak: Ah yes, I see. Sorry, Ali, you're quite right. Yes, we do need to do some more work at the whole animal level, if we want to find some technological application for this research. That's one of the reasons we're trying to get someone from the zoology department to collaborate with the group. To bring that larger perspective to things.

3.7

1 Well, for a while, people thought it could be capillary, but now it seems it's mainly …

2 So you're clear on the adhesion mechanism now, Ali?

3 That's OK. Right, so as I was saying, what I've been looking at is the effect of the geometric …

4 Anyway, because we now know that they are curved, we've …

5 Erm, could I jump in and …

4.1

Dominique: Good … so that all sounds great. You're really on track.

Silvana: Thanks.

Dominique: So I thought next maybe you could look at the adsorption of hydrogen onto some of the porous carbon materials you've been creating.

Silvana: OK, and do you have any idea about how I could do that?

Dominique: Well, I think you need to first come up with a list of the variables that could influence the uptake.

Silvana: Well, I guess what is probably most important is the porosity of the carbon fibres.

Dominique: And what would affect that?

Silvana: Well, from the work I've done so far, it seems that the temperature they were carbonised at makes a big difference to porosity – lower temperatures are better.

Dominique: OK, so one variable you could look at is carbonisation temperatures.

Silvana: So perhaps I should look at the 1273 kelvin and 973 kelvin temperatures.

Dominique: Good, so what else?

Silvana: Well, erm, actually, I'm not sure …

Dominique: Think about how you would activate the fibres.

Silvana: Activate the fibres? Ah, OK, well, from the literature I've read it's generally the case that people have been activating them with either potassium or sodium hydroxide. So I guess that could be another variable.

Dominique: Excellent. Anything else?

Silvana: Another hydroxide?

Dominique: No, that wasn't what I was thinking of.

Silvana: Erm …

Dominique: How much of the hydroxide did they use?

Silvana: Oh, er, I'm not sure actually. Sorry. It's been a while since I looked at the papers.

Dominique: Mmm …

Silvana: In fact, now I think about it, I've got a feeling they might have used different ratios. I should go back and check.

Dominique: So …

Silvana: Sorry?

Dominique: So in your next set of experiments? Variables?

Silvana: Ah … I see, I could make different ratios of hydroxide to carbon fibres another variable. Sorry, that wasn't very clever of me, was it? So anyway perhaps I could start with looking just at a couple of different ratios, say 4 to 1 and 10 to 1.

Dominique: Excellent.

Silvana: And how about looking at different heating rates … or the nitrogen flow rate? Should I vary those too?

Dominique: Hmm, ideally yes, but I think what's going to happen is you'll have too many variables and the results will become too difficult to analyse. You

might also find it difficult to reproduce the data if you change too many factors. You might be able to just look at the papers you mentioned and see what they found to be the optimal conditions, and then try to replicate those to start with. You can always adjust them later.

Silvana: OK, I'll do that, and maybe I'll have a talk to Mauritz about the adsorption protocols he's been using.

4.2

Conversation 1

A: Right, the liquid has collected in the flask.

B: So now, you can simply use litmus paper to check that it is in fact pH neutral.

A: OK … so … that looks red to me …

Conversation 2

A: And then I was going to use the geiger counter to check for radiation.

B: No, that won't work. You can't really detect gamma rays with a geiger counter. You need to use the scintillation counter for that.

A: Oh, right … but the geiger counter is OK for measuring beta radiation, right?

B: Yes, sure. For beta radiation it's fine.

Conversation 3

A: And so we record the membrane potential at a single point on the axon through the stages.

B: And how do you do that?

A: Oh, by using an oscilloscope we can create a trace of how the voltage changes through the different phases, rising, falling and undershoot. See, it produces this arc.

Conversation 4

A: Just put the sample into the spectrometer.

B: Uh-huh …

A: So this will measure the intensity of the blue-green light that passes through … and that will allow you to work out the haemoglobin concentration.

B: Right. That seems pretty straightforward.

Conversation 5

A: So we could look at BMI, but instead we're measuring body fat and we're using these calipers to do that … like this.

B: OK, so basically the distance between them is measuring the fat thickness.

A: Yeah, it's really simple.

Conversation 6

A: So you were using that piece of equipment to test the subjects' hand grip. What is it called?

B: The hand dynamometer? The one they squeeze?

A: Yeah, that one. Dynamometer? So that measures force or torque, right?

B: Yes, that's right.

Conversation 7

A: So this is a seismograph?

B: Well, actually it's a seismometer. They're both used to measure movement – motion – though.

A: So the difference is … ?

B: Well, with a seismograph you get a drawing, a trace. The seismometer just measures … it doesn't draw.

Conversation 8

A: So we can tell how smooth the surface is by measuring the interference pattern of the two waves of light.

B: OK, so you use the interferometer for that?

A: Right, for measuring the wavelengths and their interference when they encounter one another.

■■■ **4.3**

Silvana: Mauritz, do you have time to talk to me about your adsorption protocols? Dominique suggested that I talk to you.

Mauritz: Sure, just let me set this … OK, so what is it you're going to be doing?

Silvana: OK, well, I've been working on a plan for the activation of carbon fibres. I'm going to start off with fibres which have been carbonised at two different temperatures. And then I'm going to activate each one with either potassium or sodium hydroxide, at two different ratios. And then after that I'll look at hydrogen adsorption.

Mauritz: Sounds good. OK, so first you would need to do the activation.

Silvana: Yeah. I was thinking of simply mixing the fibres with the hydroxides in pellet form, at the relevant ratios.

Mauritz: Ratios based on weight or volume?

Silvana: Oh, weight of course.

Mauritz: Just checking!

Silvana: I think the literature suggests 2 grammes of fibres with the relevant amount of hydroxide, so I think I'll try using those quantities first.

Mauritz: OK, so what ratios are you going to use?

Silvana: 4:1 and 10:1. But then they need to be heated …

Mauritz: OK, fine. And have you thought about the set-up for that?

Silvana: Yeah, a little bit. Here's a quick sketch I made of what I was thinking of. On the inside, I thought I should have the sample on a tray in an inner tube.

Mauritz: The tray's steel?

Silvana: Mmm, yes. Or ceramic. I'm not sure yet, but I figure as long as it's unreactive it should be OK.

Mauritz: I guess, but if I were you, I'd use steel. The ceramic trays tend to be a bit bigger.

Silvana: OK, thanks. And then the inner tube is surrounded by a tube furnace, which you can see here.

Mauritz: Uh-huh.

Silvana: But I'm not sure what the tube should be made from, or even sizes for that matter.

Mauritz: I know someone who used to do something similar to this. She had a, maybe metre and a half, quartz tube, but it was quite narrow, less than 10 centimetres. I'd guess at maybe 6 to 7.5 centimetres across. Why don't you try that to start with?

Silvana: Sure. So, I'll just note those dimensions down – 1.5 metres and 10 centimetres.

Mauritz: No, I'd use less than 10 centimetres. Between 6 and 7.5.

Silvana: Oh, OK. So then the furnace needs to be linked to a temperature controller. That's up here.

Mauritz: And doesn't heating rate play a role here?

Silvana: Yes, it does. But Dominique suggested picking just one rate initially. The papers I've looked at suggest 5 kelvins a minute, up to 1025 kelvins, and then constant for an hour, so I'm planning to stick with that.

Mauritz: Hmm, personally I think slightly longer would be better. I think you should maintain the temperature for 75 minutes.

Silvana: Great. OK, so I'll go for 75 minutes at temperature.

Mauritz: And then it just cools naturally?

Silvana: I think so. I haven't included any cooling apparatus here, so I'll try relying on natural convection first, and if it doesn't work, I can add some kind of cooling mechanism later on.

Mauritz: Great. So what's this on the left?

Silvana: That's the nitrogen cylinder. There'll be a constant flow of nitrogen. I was planning on running it through at 500 mils a minute, through the entire heat treatment.

Mauritz: Well, it really sounds like you have that all worked out. It looks like it should work. And you have the washing and drying figured out?

Silvana: Yeah, again from what I've read, the best thing to do …

■■■ **4.4**

Silvana: Here's a quick sketch I made of what I was thinking of. On the inside, I thought I should have the sample on a tray in an inner tube.

Mauritz: The tray's steel?

Silvana: Mmm yes. Or ceramic. I'm not sure yet, but I figure as long as it's unreactive it should be OK.

Mauritz: I guess, but if I were you, I'd use steel. The ceramic trays tend to be a bit bigger.

Silvana: OK, thanks. And then the inner tube is surrounded by a tube furnace, which you can see here.

Mauritz: Uh-huh.

Silvana: But I'm not sure what the tube should be made from, or even sizes for that matter.

Mauritz: I know someone who used to do something similar to this. She had a, maybe metre and a half, quartz tube, but it was quite narrow, less than 10 centimetres. I'd guess at maybe 6 to 7.5 centimetres across. Why don't you try that to start with?

Silvana: Sure. So, I'll just note those dimensions down – 1.5 metres and 10 centimetres.

Mauritz: No, I'd use less than 10 centimetres. Between 6 and 7.5.

Silvana: Oh, OK. So then the furnace needs to be linked to a temperature controller. That's up here.

Mauritz: And doesn't heating rate play a role here?

Silvana: Yes, it does. But Dominique suggested picking just one rate initially. The papers I've looked at suggest 5 kelvins a minute, up to 1025 kelvins, and then constant for an hour, so I'm planning to stick with that.

Mauritz: Hmm, personally I think slightly longer would be better. I think you should maintain the temperature for 75 minutes.

Silvana: Great. OK, so I'll go for 75 minutes at temperature.

Mauritz: And then it just …

■■■ **4.5**

Silvana: … I've done a bit more reading, going back to some papers I read at the start and looking a bit more at the detail, and I've had a talk to Mauritz, and to Padma, about the protocols, so I think I'm basically ready to go now.

Dominique: OK, so let's talk through what you think might happen, from what you've read.

Silvana: Well …

Dominique: Start with what you know best, the carbonisation temperatures.

Silvana: OK, so from what I've been doing, I know that carbonisation temperature has an effect on porosity.

Dominique: Uh-huh …

Silvana: And so if lower temperatures increase porosity, the fibres which are carbonised at lower temperatures will probably adsorb more hydrogen.

Dominique: That makes sense. So the next variable was going to be which hydroxide you use. Any idea what will happen there?

Silvana: Well, I really don't expect there to be any difference between the sodium and potassium hydroxides.

Dominique: Oh …

Silvana: Well, I mean, I don't know that, it's just a guess, but I don't expect a difference because they both seem to be pretty good activators from what I've read. Saying that though, I haven't found any literature which compares the two directly. I'm actually really interested to see if there is a difference.

Dominique: Yes, that should be interesting. And the ratios?

Silvana: Hmm, well, my prediction is that the higher ratio will lead to better activation of the fibres and I think better activation will allow more adsorption. But actually, I've been thinking about this a lot and I'm wondering if I should do a wider variety of ratios – maybe add in a 6 to 1, giving three variables there. What do you think?

Dominique: I can see how it would be useful, but I think to start with you should concentrate on just the two, while you perfect the method, and then you can fill in the gaps later.

Silvana: OK, I'll stick with just the two for a start.

Dominique: And hopefully you'll have some data ready for when I get back from my trip. We can meet again then to look at it.

▬ 5.1

Chuyu: … I've just finished writing it, so could you look at it before I show Lucia?

Thabo: Of course. So it's a summary of the way the multi-anvil works?

Chuyu: Kind of. It's the process I use to measure the mineral strength, so yes, including the multi-anvil.

Thabo: Right. OK. Well, the first thing I can see is that you need to make sure you use linking words, to make your stages clear.

Chuyu: Do you mean things like firstly, secondly? Well that should be easy enough.

Thabo: Yes, some of those, but also things like 'then', 'after that' and all those kinds of sequence words.

Chuyu: Right, OK.

Thabo: Not too many, though. And you might find that when you do that your sentences seem a little short, and the language could be a bit repetitive.

Chuyu: So I need to find other words to say the same thing?

Thabo: Well, you could do, but I was thinking more that you will need to combine sentences.

Chuyu: Can you give me an example?

Thabo: Mmm. So here, in the second and third sentences, you've got 'The powdered mineral sample was placed into a tube of rolled rhenium. The rhenium tube was loaded into a ceramic octahedron.'

Chuyu: Yes …

Thabo: So it would be better to say 'First … the powdered mineral sample was placed into a tube of rolled rhenium, *which* was *then* loaded into a ceramic octahedron.'

Chuyu: Ah, I see. So this one would be …

▬ 5.2

Thabo: Well, you could do, but I was thinking more that you will need to combine sentences.

Chuyu: Can you give me an example?

Thabo: Mmm. So here, in the second and third sentences, you've got 'The powdered mineral sample was placed into a tube of rolled rhenium. The rhenium tube was loaded into a ceramic octahedron.'

Chuyu: Yes …

Thabo: So it would be better to say 'First … the powdered mineral sample was placed into a tube of rolled rhenium, *which* was *then* loaded into a ceramic octahedron.'

Chuyu: Ah, I see. So this one would be …

▬ 5.3

Chuyu: So let me tell you about my results, and then we can have a look at yours.

Lucia: So what did you find?

Chuyu: Well, so far, I've looked at the upper mantle olivine and the lower mantle perovskite. And then I've also done a couple of runs with wadsleyite and ringwoodite from the transition zone, but I'm having some issues … I'm getting weird and inconsistent results.

Lucia: Well tell me about the ones you're happy with for a start, and then we can try to work out what's going on with the others. So?

Chuyu: Right, well, firstly I thought that the differential stress in all of the samples would go up as the pressure increased … and it *did* for olivine and for perovskite. In fact, there was a clear linear relationship until the sample yielded. Then it reached a plateau.

Lucia: So the differential stress after that is actually the yield strength of the sample.

Chuyu: Right. And, as I expected, the perovskite was the strongest. It yielded later than olivine.

Lucia: Uh-huh.

Chuyu: But what was really interesting though was when the samples were also heated.

Lucia: In what way?

Chuyu: OK, well, I expected that increasing the temperature would reduce yield strength.

Lucia: So the mineral would yield at a lower pressure if the temperature increased?

Chuyu: Right. And that's what did happen with the olivine. In fact, its strength went right down as the temperature went up.

Lucia: By how much?

Chuyu: Well, when the pressure was maintained at 10 gigapascals, increasing the temperature to 873 kelvins reduced the yield strength to less than a fifth of what it was at ambient temperature.

Lucia: A fifth? Wow, that's pretty amazing.

Chuyu: Yes, but possibly more surprising was that the perovskite seemed resistant to temperature. Even increasing the temperature at high pressure didn't reduce yield strength.

Lucia: Really? I thought the minerals would all be affected by temperature. I mean to some degree, at least.

Chuyu: Well that's what I expected too, but it seems I was wrong …

▬ 5.4

Lucia: Really? I thought the minerals would all be affected by temperature. I mean to some degree, at least.

Chuyu: Well that's what I expected too, but it seems I was wrong. I guess there are a couple of possibilities. The first is that the sample needs to be heated to an even higher temperature … I've gone up to 873 kelvins but perhaps what I need to do in the next run is increase the temperature even more. I can get it up to 1073 kelvins without any trouble but I'm not sure I can go any further.

Lucia: Uh-huh.

Chuyu: Another possibility is that the pressure needs to increase. Perhaps with a higher pressure, temperature would have an effect.

Lucia: But you can't get it any higher, can you?

Chuyu: I can, but I would need to use the Diamond-anvil cell to do that.

Lucia: OK. And is there another possibility?

Chuyu: Yes, that this is a real result. I've run the experiment numerous times with a few different samples and the results I'm getting really do seem to suggest that the yield strength of perovskite is unresponsive to temperature.

▬ 5.5

Chuyu: But then the ringwoodite. It's a transition zone mineral, so I expect it to act like wadsleyite.

Lucia: So again, kind of halfway between olivine and perovskite?

Chuyu: Mmm. But it's causing me no end of problems. I mean, I haven't done much with it, but so far the results are all over the place. Look.

Lucia: Mmm, I see what you mean. That doesn't look too good.

Chuyu: Not too good? It's a disaster!

Lucia: So what do you think is going wrong?

Chuyu: Well, I've got a couple of ideas.

Lucia: Yes?

Chuyu: Well, firstly, the samples I've been using might not be ringwoodite at all.

Lucia: How so?

Chuyu: Well, look at this set of results.

Lucia: Hmm. It looks like you're using olivine again. Could the samples have been switched by accident, maybe?

Chuyu: Well, maybe. But I doubt it's olivine. But it could be something else very similar. Forsterite, maybe?

Lucia: Yeah, it's possible. But I really think it's unlikely.

Chuyu: Yeah, I do too. But I've sent it off for a composition analysis anyway. Just to rule it out. So my second idea is—

Lucia: Hang on. I'm sure I remember Thabo talking about strange results just like this a few months ago. He reckoned the machine needed recalibrating. Maybe that's the problem.

Chuyu: Mmm, yes, I guess if my measurements aren't coming from the same base point then there could be problems. But I'm sure there were technicians here just a couple of weeks ago checking and adjusting it.

Lucia: You could be right. It was just a thought.

Chuyu: Mmm. But actually, now you mention it, a calibration issue is a possibility. I have to admit that I'm not the most careful about properly recalibrating between runs. I mean, I usually reset and adjust it before I start a series, but I don't always do it between every sample. I kind of figure it shouldn't get too far from standard.

Lucia: Chuyu!

Chuyu: Yeah, now you mention it …

▬▬ 5.6

A: So to assess the reaction to CO_2, I used 5 miligrams of char in the TGA pan.

B: Uh-huh, and the same heating rate as last time?

A: No, this time I heated it from room temperature to 378 kelvins.

B: Sorry, let me jot that down. Room temp. to 378 kelvins.

A: Yeah, and then held for 30 minutes.

B: 30? So that's a change from last time. It was just 20 minutes before.

A: That's right. OK, so then I heated at 20 kelvins a minute to 873 kelvins and then reduced it to 7 kelvins a minute to 1473 kelvins.

B: Great, so 20 kelvins a minute then down to 7 kelvins a minute. And the gas you used?

A: Well, it was a mixture of high purity CO_2 and nitrogen.

B: And the CO_2 concentration?

A: Oh, erm, 25% I think … let me check … yeah, 25%.

▬▬ 5.7

Chuyu: So, Mayumi, I've been thinking about switching to an e-notebook, but I've never seen anyone use one. How is it?

Mayumi: Oh, it's so much easier. But really? People here don't use them? I had to use one in my last lab, for the security. It's excellent. You should try one.

Chuyu: Ah yes. That was a commercial lab, wasn't it? I'm not surprised that the security was much tighter there.

Mayumi: But it would work really well here, too. If you have e-notebooks, everyone can share their information so easily. You don't have any problems trying to read someone else's notes.

Chuyu: Yes, and I guess you can also share things with people in other labs instantly, instead of waiting for meetings … or to write something up.

Mayumi: Yes, it's even better than sending an email because they can see everything all at once – the protocols, all the data, images, everything is there together. And another thing that's really great is that you can search your own lab book, and also if you refer to a particular compound or reagent, you can link to its details on the web. You don't have to note all its details down yourself.

Chuyu: Yes, and you don't need to worry about rules for crossing things out or leaving empty spaces or being sure to date everything. I assume that's all done automatically, you know, like the highlighting of the changes you've made?

Mayumi: That's right.

Chuyu: It sounds great in theory … but I guess the packages are set up in one particular way. It might not really be good for the research you're doing.

Mayumi: Well, that's true, but in most cases you can customise the book to your group's specifications … although that's a bit more of a problem here than it was in my last lab.

Chuyu: Hmm. But from a security point of view, it's just so much safer. There's no risk of leaving your lab book on the train.

Mayumi: When we were using paper books, we were never allowed to take them out of the lab … ever. In fact, they couldn't even be left on your desk at night. They had to go into a safe.

Chuyu: Mmm, I guess security really was much tighter there.

▬▬ 5.8

1 I had to use one in my last lab, for the security.

2 You should try one.

3 If you have e-notebooks, everyone can share their information so easily.

4 You don't need to worry about rules for crossing things out.

5 When we were using paper books, we were never allowed to take them out of the lab … ever.

▬▬ 6.1

Kimiko: Hi, Tom. Do you have a moment?

Tom: Sure, Kimiko. What can I do for you?

Kimiko: Erm … I'm just trying to write up my paper and, erm, I wondered if you could look through it for me?

Tom: Sure. I've got a bit of time now, as it goes. Was there anything in particular you wanted me to look at?

Kimiko: Not really. It's my first draft, so just any advice you could give me would be really helpful.

Tom: Sure. Let's have a look then. Well, the diagram's nice and clear.

Kimiko: Really? Oh, thanks.

Tom: But first of all you need to explain briefly what's happening, what you did, in each stage.

Kimiko: Is the diagram not clear enough?

Tom: The diagram's much clearer if you know something about the process. But not everyone who reads this paper will, so you should definitely include a short description.

Kimiko: OK. I'd better do that, then.

Tom: Why don't you talk me through it and make some notes as you go? Then you can write it up properly later.

Kimiko: Thanks, Tom. So, the basic idea is that we can use carbon nanotubes, CNTs, to send a drug right to where it's needed. That's why some people call it a 'magic bullet'.

Tom: Uh-huh.

Kimiko: To do this, first we coat the surface of the tube with a chemical receptor. For instance, if we want to target a tumour which overexpresses folic acid, then we attach folate receptors to the surface of the nanotube.

Tom: Because folate receptors bind to folic acid?

Kimiko: Yes. And then we encapsulate the drug in the tube. This is the part I'm most interested in. Up to now, a lot of different methods to get things into the cell have been tried, but I'm looking at just one of them in my paper. OK, so if you look here at the first part of the diagram … once the drug is encapsulated, we use a cap to close the open end so the drug can't escape.

Tom: And that's when we take the capsules?

Kimiko: Yes. You can swallow them or you could have them injected, or even inhaled.

Tom: OK. So then they're in the body, shooting to the target?

Kimiko: Uh-huh, and if they're properly functionalised, they should arrive. After that, the capsule is internalised by the cell.

Tom: And how does that happen?

Kimiko: Through receptor-mediated endocytosis. Then the tube opens up in order to let the drug out. There are different ways of doing this, but I use biodegradable caps. The cap dissolves and then …

Tom: And then the drug can start doing its work?

Kimiko: Exactly … it's released from the tube and starts to act.

Tom: Well, that sounds fine so far, Kimiko. If I were you, I'd write that up first.

Kimiko: And then can I get you to look at the rest?

Tom: Sure, no problem.

Kimiko: Thanks, Tom. I'll see you later.

■ 6.2

1 To do this, first we coat the surface of the tube with a chemical receptor.
2 If we want to target a tumour which overexpresses folic acid, then we attach folate receptors to the surface of the nanotube.
3 And then we encapsulate the drug in the tube.
4 Once the drug is encapsulated, we use a cap to close the open end so the drug can't escape.
5 After that, the capsule is internalised by the cell.
6 I use biodegradable caps. The cap dissolves and then …

■ 6.3

Tom: OK, so—
Kimiko: Oh my goodness! Look at all that underlining! My English is so terrible!
Tom: Oh Kimiko! No, no, it's fine! Really!
Kimiko: But …
Tom: I was looking at style, rather than grammar, the grammar's fine. Just look at all the parts I *haven't* underlined! Look, this first sentence is really nice. It gives a really good overview of the aim of the whole process.
Kimiko: OK …
Tom: OK, so, style: like here I noticed that you've used too many sequencing words. It's OK to use some but you've got firstly, secondly … even fifth. I used to do the same thing. It's better to just write in order and only use words like 'then' when you really need to. You'll get more natural at it in time. So I'd cut all those words if I were you.
Kimiko: Maybe as I read more papers I'll write better.
Tom: Definitely, definitely. OK, the next thing is that you've said 'I functionalise the surface'. Remember to keep the writing objective. It shouldn't matter who does the experiment, the result should be the same. So don't use 'I' or 'We' in your write-up.
Kimiko: So what should I say instead?
Tom: Use passives instead. So here 'The surface of the nanotubes *is* functionalised'. You see what I mean about style? Actually, there is just one, literally one, grammar mistake though. You've said '*for* target a tumour which da-da-da' but it should be '*to* target'. You use 'to' and the verb to say *why* you do something.
Kimiko: Oh!
Tom: Hey, come on – one mistake is really pretty good.
Kimiko: I guess. What about this one? It should say 'the drug molecules *were* encapsulated' not 'I encapsulated', right?
Tom: Erm, where are we? Oh yes. Yes, yes, it should be passive. But it should also be in the *present* tense, not the past.

Kimiko: But why? I thought when I talked about an experiment I'd done, I should use the past.
Tom: Well, that's true, but here you're talking about the process in *general*. It's not about one particular experiment you've done.
Kimiko: Right. So, the general process is in the present, but when I go on to focus on my experiments, on filling the nanotubes, I should use the past.
Tom: Exactly right. Like here, 'the nanotubes are ingested'. I'd take out this sentence though – the examples of the ways to ingest the tubes. I mean it's true, but it's not really relevant to the focus of your research. Never include information the reader doesn't need to understand your work. Even if it's interesting.
Kimiko: OK. Then this next sentence should be passive, I guess. 'The target site is located by the nanotube'.
Tom: Well, actually, no. Your original sentence is fine. Some verbs can have a non-human subject, so you don't need to use passive. Like 'locate to' here, or 'internalises' in the next sentence. 'The target cell internalises the nanotube' is completely fine.
Kimiko: Er … so why have you underlined it?
Tom: Well, it's fine if you're talking about target cells. But in your text you've been talking about nanotubes all the time, so that should be your subject.
Kimiko: So I should use passive, then? To bring 'nanotubes' to the beginning of the sentence.
Tom: Exactly.
Kimiko: OK, and this last one should be 'the nanotube is internalised by da-da-da'?
Tom: Ha-ha! Right! So anyway let's have a look …

■ 6.4

1 As this was a dosage of 0.166 miligrams of fluoride per kilogram body weight, the equivalent amount needed to achieve a similar peak in a 20 kilogram child would be 3.33 miligrams of fluoride.
2 The sensitivity of the assay was 0.2 picomoles.
3 The output impedance is about 0.02 ohms at the 5 volt end and 0.1 ohm at the 15 volt end of the range.
4 Six-amp three-core mains flex is used for the mains input which connects straight to the p.c.b.
5 Inserting a few atoms of potassium makes the compound a superconductor which, below a critical temperature of about 19 kelvins, conducts electricity with no resistance.
6 This shows that where two moles of hydrogen gas combine with one mole of oxygen gas to form two moles of liquid water, at a pressure of one atmosphere and a temperature of 298 kelvins, the enthalpy change is minus 571.6 kilojoules.

7 Isolated young mice squeak repeatedly at frequencies of 45 kilohertz to 88 kilohertz, until their mother comes and returns them to the nest.
8 In a similar form of these experiments, conventional, 50-nanosecond laser pulses were used.

■ 6.5

a A quarter
b Fifteen percent
c One point three five six
d Two million, nine hundred and five thousand, seven hundred and forty
e Five times ten to the nine
f Minus thirty-five
g Ten to the power of six
h Ten thousand, eight hundred and ninety-three
i Minus fifty-seven
j Seventeen and five eighths
k Nought point nought nought three
l Five million, ninety thousand and nineteen

■ 6.6

1
a three quarters
b five eighths
c four ninths
d ten to the power of seven
e ten to the power of minus nine

2
a per cent
b times
c minus

3
one point three five six … one thousand, three hundred and fifty-six

■ 6.7

Arnie: So, you were more successful this time, Kimiko. Run me through what you did. And particularly what you did differently.
Kimiko: So, this time I think the tubes I used were more consistent in size. 20–50 micrometres in length, with an average diameter of 500 nanometres and the wall thickness was—
Arnie: Ah, sorry, if we could just go back a moment. The average diameter was 500 nanometres. So what was the range exactly?
Kimiko: The range, yes, uh, the EM images showed them being between 300 and 700 nanometres, but sometimes the tubes get deformed so they might have been slightly narrower than that.
Arnie: Hmm. See if you can get that even more standardised next time, if possible.
Kimiko: OK. I'll just make a note of that.
Arnie: And the wall thickness?
Kimiko: Erm … on the 29th it was 20 nanometres, but this time it was a bit less, at 15 nanometres.
Arnie: Right, so last time you had problems getting the tubes onto the slides. That went better this time?

Kimiko: Yes, much. I suspended the tubes in the 2-propanol and then used dielectrophoresis to get them onto the slide. The 2-propanol just dries away.

Arnie: And that worked?

Kimiko: Yes, really well.

Arnie: OK, so we don't need to change anything there.

Kimiko: No, not at all. So after that, just like last time, I put a drop of the beads suspended in ethylene glycol at one end of the tube. The beads were the same as before – 50-nanometre diameter – but this time I used 1 to 3 beads to liquid instead of 1 to 1 like last time.

Arnie: Aha!

Kimiko: And this time I used the glass micropipette, as you suggested … and then I dipped the end of the tube in the drop and it just filled the tube. Just by capillary action.

Arnie: So we were right. It can be done that way.

Kimiko: It seems so. And after the liquid evaporated, we had plenty of beads still in the tube.

Arnie: Great. So what now?

Kimiko: Well, I think that the overall length of the tube maybe affects the filling rate, and it might also depend how much of the tube is in the solution. I'm not sure, but I guess ideally I'd look at that next.

Arnie: That sounds like a good idea. Let me know how you get on.

▉ 7.1

Nour: So what is it that you work on, Tiago? Océane didn't really explain to me.

Tiago: Oh, right. Well, I'm looking at how shrimp have adapted to the hydrothermal vent environment. To the high temperatures and the metal concentrations.

Nour: Shrimp. Right. And what are you measuring? I mean, how do they adapt?

Tiago: Oh, so I've been looking at metallothionein levels.

Nour: And they are the metal-binding proteins, right?

Tiago: Yes, exactly. So I'm expecting vent shrimp to show higher levels, to be able to deal with the high concentrations. Oh, I should have said, I'm comparing two vent species from the Rainbow field and two lagoon species from the Rio Formosa lagoon. They're, like, my control.

Nour: Right. And are you looking at antioxidants as well? They're usually important, aren't they?

Tiago: Yes, yes I am. Four different types of antioxidant enzyme.

Nour: And how is it going? What are your results looking like?

Tiago: Oh, well, I've collected quite a lot of raw data and I've just started doing my analysis. But I'm getting some interesting results. Anyway, what is it you're focusing on, Nour?

▉ 7.2

Océane: OK, so let's have a look at these charts.

Tiago: Which do you want to start with? There are a lot.

Océane: Well, as they're all bar charts so far, let's look at the MT one first and then any changes we make to it can probably be made on the others too, I expect.

Tiago: OK, here it is.

Océane: Right, so your scale is good, the chart looks a good size.

Tiago: And for the antioxidant levels, is it OK to have different scales?

Océane: Yes, of course. Imagine how it would look otherwise. Right, but what you haven't done is label your axes. You need to do that.

Tiago: So just with what it measures? MT levels on the y-axis and the location on the x, or do I need the species?

Océane: Hang on. Remember that the units for the MT levels also need to be included.

Tiago: So I need to say the MT level, milligrams per gram of protein?

Océane: Right. If that's what your unit is.

Tiago: Yeah.

Océane: Now, the shading you have used is good. It'll reproduce well in print.

Tiago: And I've made sure they're consistent across all the graphs.

Océane: Great. But you do need to have a key, to show what your colours mean. I know you've put that in the caption, but a key is essential all the same.

Tiago: OK, that's not a problem. I'll add a key to each one.

Océane: OK, something else you need to add to your charts is an indication of your standard deviation. I assume what you've plotted is the mean?

Tiago: Yes. So I should add those 'T's on top of the bars?

Océane: Yes, that's certainly one effective way of doing it. And you've already highlighted those results that are not statistically significant. That's great, Tiago.

Tiago: Thanks.

Océane: Just make sure you mention that that's what it shows in the caption.

Tiago: OK, I will. And while we're on the subject of captions …

▉ 7.3

Nour: So Océane, there's something I don't understand. Why do I need to write descriptions of my charts in the results section if they can stand alone?

Océane: That's true, they do stand alone. But the text highlights the *key* results. A chart might show a few different things; the text points out which are the most important.

Nour: OK, that makes sense. And another thing, what about results I wasn't expecting? If I have negative results, should I include those?

Océane: Definitely, I mean, they're an important part of finding the answer to your questions.

Nour: Right, well I have a couple of those. So then do I need to say what the results mean here? Or is that in the discussion?

Océane: No, no, no. In this section, you should just highlight the main trends of key differences. Any interpretation comes in the discussion section, as you said.

Nour: Good, that's what I thought. OK, so in the results section, do I need to put in every table or chart that I've produced?

Océane: No, because some of your charts will not really show anything of interest. Look, what I would do is this. First, take all your charts and choose which ones show important findings. Then, decide which order you should describe them in to present your results logically.

Nour: OK, so choose them, then order them. And number them then?

Océane: Yes. Remember – tables and figures are numbered separately.

Nour: Yeah.

Océane: While you're working out the order, make a note of what the key results depicted in the charts are. Look at getting a couple of points for each chart. They're what you talk about in the results section.

Nour: OK, so do I need to write about all the visuals I include in the paper?

Océane: Yes. Any table or graph which is shown in the paper also needs an explanation in the text of the results section.

Nour: Right. And in the same order they're numbered too, I guess?

Océane: Yes.

Nour: So this might be a silly question, but what kind of things are key results?

Océane: Well, in general, you're looking at things that are interesting because they're similar, or because they're different. You might have values that are very high or low … or interesting correlations.

Nour: Hmm, right … and then when I'm describing a figure, do I need to mention every value?

Océane: Absolutely not. As I said, make notes on the key results only. Another thing to remember is that you shouldn't include raw numbers. You can talk about means, about percentages, that's OK, and remember to include units. People sometimes forget.

Nour: And should I include my statistics?

Océane: Well, one mistake people often make is to use whole sentences to talk about the statistics. What you should do is put the test name and the p-value in parentheses after the result.

8.1

Max: OK, so what I'm trying to do is to dope graphene to make it more useful for electronics.

Florence: Right, so when we dope silicon we add boron, phosphorus, something like that, actually into the crystal structure to change its properties. Are you doing the same?

Max: Well, yes and no. I mean, of course I'm adding something to try to change its properties.

Florence: But?

Max: But because the graphene is really just an ultra-thin layer of carbon, I'm trying to just put the dopant onto the sheet.

Florence: And you're using … ?

Max: Well, I've tried gold and nitrogen dioxide, but I've only had mixed results. So recently I've been working with F4-TCNQ.

Florence: Ah, right.

Max: So really I've been trying to work out a couple of things. First, I just needed to see if doping graphene with F4-TCNQ could neutralise the excess negative charge.

Florence: Mmm …

Max: I mean, it certainly seemed theoretically and experimentally possible, but it hadn't been done.

Florence: And it worked?

Max: Yeah, it seems to have. I'll let you have a look at some of the data to see what you think.

Florence: Sure! That'd be great. And did you look at the stability of the dopant?

Max: Yeah, that was the second thing. Really, it was whether it was air and temperature resistant that I was initially interested in. But I have a couple of other ideas now.

Florence: It sounds really interesting. I'd love to look at the draft when it's ready.

8.2

Florence: So some things that you need to remember when writing the results section are, well, first, as I said when I looked at the draft paragraph, you should only present the results. Without any interpretation, without any methodology.

Max: Yes, I've got that now.

Florence: OK, so the next thing to think about is being sure you highlight both your key findings … and any secondary ones, too. People sometimes only put in the main finding, but there's often more which is interesting.

Max: Great, so how do I order them?

Florence: OK, so what I'd do is prepare the figures and tables, to summarise the data … and then basically think about the most logical order to present that data. That's the order your results section should follow. Or at least that's how I do it.

Max: Follow the order of the visuals, right. That's good advice.

Florence: Yeah, so it's like writing a story. It kind of develops step by step. First step, then second step based on the results found in the first step, and so on. It's also helpful to paragraph your text so that each paragraph is clearly related to one of your research questions, or a part of your research question.

Max: So I'd have, say, one paragraph about the stability of the layer in air, another about its reaction to temperature? Is that what you mean?

Florence: Yes, exactly. And make sure in your text that you include references to the relevant visuals.

Max: So by saying 'figure 1', 'table 2', things like that.

Florence: Yes, phrases like 'as shown in figure 1' are really useful.

Max: And language tips?

Florence: Oh, well, being concise – not using too many words – is the thing I find most difficult. Erm, what else? Oh, I usually end up with lots of passives, but Dan always says to include as much active voice as possible.

Max: Right, so different to the method.

Florence: Mmm, yeah. And use past tenses. Oh, and something else he says is try not to be repetitive in your structures. I often do that.

Max: Right, that's great, Florence. Thanks.

Florence: One last thing. It is OK to use subheadings, if it makes things clearer – for example, if you have done a few experiments and have a few different sets of results.

Max: Oh, right. I didn't know that. I don't think I'll need headings, but I'll keep it in mind.

8.3

Max: So, my discussion section should explain how my results relate to my hypothesis; what they mean?

Florence: Yes, so for example you could talk about how the fluorine groups are important for electron transfer. That would be an interpretation.

Max: OK. So, in terms of the order – should I work through my discussion in the same order I used for the results?

Florence: Yeah, definitely. You need to basically comment on all the results you mentioned, in the same order, and say what they mean.

Max: And can I mention any new results in this part? Or just the ones I've already written about in the results section?

Florence: If it's a result worth mentioning, it should be in the results.

Max: And do I need to mention the results again? I assume not, but don't I need to remind the reader what the results were, before I interpret them?

Florence: Well, that's a tricky one. You certainly don't need to mention all the results in detail, but you're right, you might need to make a reference to them.

Max: So how can I include that information, but without repetition?

Florence: Well, you can use noun phrases. That's a quick and easy way to sum up your results without having to describe them all over again.

Max: Right, I see. So I'm not actually repeating the results, more summarising them further. And can I refer to other work that's been done in the area?

Florence: Oh sure. It's good to tie your work in to what others say to support your interpretation. Or to other work you've done.

Max: And in terms of language, is there anything in particular I should be careful with?

Florence: Well, the most difficult thing I think is being concise; not using too many words. But that's always a problem for me too, actually.

8.4

Dan: Yes, this looks good, Max, but I think you should add a short section on limitations and your future plans.

Max: And that's part of the discussion?

Dan: Yes, just a paragraph at the end is fine. Just before your concluding paragraph.

Max: So what kind of thing would I say?

Dan: OK, well one of the things you mentioned here is that increasing the annealing temperature seems to cause desorption.

Max: Yes, above 75 degrees.

Dan: Yes, but it could be that annealing in a vacuum is playing a role. I mean, it may well be that you need higher temperatures at atmospheric pressure to remove the layer.

Max: Oh, yeah. I'd thought about that but I thought if I mentioned it I should really do the experiment.

Dan: But then you'd never get the paper done … and it would be a very long paper if you covered all the possibilities. No, it's fine to say that's something to be looked at, but start doing it as soon as possible, before someone else does it.

Max: All right. So another thing that's maybe a problem is that I can't get the graphene samples totally consistent. You can tell from the spectroscopy data that there are slightly different thicknesses.

Dan: Mmm.

Max: I don't think it's a big issue, and I'm not sure how to get around it, but it is a bit of a problem.

Dan: Well, perhaps … but I think it's basically inevitable.

Max: Yeah.

Dan: So, do you have any other ideas for extending the work?

Max: Oh, absolutely. Something else I want to do is look at a way of applying the F4-TCNQ layer. This time, I used evaporation, but I'm wondering if we could just dip the sample in an F4-TCNQ solution.

Dan: Yes, it's worth a try.

Max: Yeah, I think so. I mean, if it works you'd be able to take a ready-made graphene object, dip it in the solution and alter its electronic properties. It's definitely got potential.

▬▬ 9.1

Svenja: That all looks good, Mya. You've really done a good job. Now, the abstract.

Mya: OK, here it is. So basically what I did was take the most important sentences from each of the sections and put them in order.

Svenja: Yes, that's a good way to start. As you write more, you'll be able to write the abstract independently, but that's a good technique at first.

Mya: Oh, good.

Svenja: So, here you have a nice clear background to the topic. That's a good first sentence. But you should never reference other people's work in an abstract.

Mya: Really? But if I don't refer to other work, doesn't that make my work seem less relevant? Less credible?

Svenja: No, not at all. You'll reference them in the introduction. The abstract should be very general – not focused on particular evidence.

Mya: Right. Just in the introduction and discussion then.

Svenja: Well, mainly there, yes. All right … so next you mention your research question … good … that's a nice clear phrase to use.

Mya: Oh, good.

Svenja: And you've narrowed things down to which kind of protective condition you are looking at. Oh, but don't go into so much detail here. I mean, is it really the composition of the surface which has an effect?

Mya: Oh, erm … I don't know.

Svenja: Well, just leave the first part and take away from 'due to the fact' onwards.

Mya: OK, so next I've summarised the method.

Svenja: That's good, and you have another good introductory phrase there … but you have included way too much detail. All this about the composition, temperature and radiation can go.

Mya: Yes, I guess if someone wants to know all that detail, they can read the method.

Svenja: OK, next problem is you've got a reference to your figures here.

Mya: Yeah, the line graphs of exposure time and growth.

Svenja: Don't include references to figures in the abstract either.

Mya: Right … and how about the language, is that OK?

▬▬ 9.2

Mya: So, I have a few ideas for titles sketched out, but I don't know which is best.

Svenja: OK, let's have a look then. Right, well, this first one, 'Is there life on Mars?', is no good.

Mya: Yeah, I didn't think it would really be suitable, but I thought it was good to have something catchy, jokey though, with a fun reference.

Svenja: Well, I don't know if that's true really. Look at it this way, will all your intended audience understand the reference you're making? If they do, well, they'll chuckle … but if they don't get the joke, all you're left with is an extremely vague title.

Mya: That's true, I guess.

Svenja: And looked at another way, who is going to find it when they're searching the online journals?

Mya: Well, someone who searches 'life' and 'Mars'?

Svenja: But would someone in the field search for such vague terms? Your title needs to contain the important keywords that someone would search for – otherwise it won't be found.

Mya: OK, so how about my second one: 'Are there any features on Mars that could provide protection against the harsh surface conditions?'? It's got the idea of Mars, protection, the harsh conditions …

Svenja: Yes, that's true, but it's still rather vague. It seems that what you've done here is just use your research question as your title.

Mya: I thought that would be a good idea. I mean, that tells people what I was looking at.

Svenja: Yes, but that title could have been written before you did the research … and anyone can ask a question. What you can do now though, after your studies, is give us an answer to the question. So instead of using the question you asked as your title, write a statement telling the reader what your key result was. That's much more informative.

Mya: So this one – 'An investigation into whether Mars's surface material could provide protection for organisms' – is better. It explains the key finding. I mean, it kind of sums up the content.

Svenja: Well, it does to an extent, but it's still a little imprecise. Protection for organisms? For dogs? Cats? Humans?

Mya: For some organisms?

Svenja: Why not tell us which ones? It's often good to include details like the species studied, or if you're focusing on one field location, the place – things like that are important. Also protection. Protection from the rain? Say what they're protected from.

Mya: Oh. I thought it would be confusing if I used too many technical terms.

Svenja: Yes, you're right, being too technical isn't good – but this isn't jargon, it's detail. And again, 'an investigation into' tells us what you did, not what you found. Try to avoid starting with phrases like 'an observation of' or 'a study of'. Your next suggestion 'Protection for *Acidithiobacillus ferrooxidans* and *Deinococcus radiodurans* exposed to simulated Mars environmental conditions by surface material' is much, much better.

Mya: But a bit too long?

Svenja: No, I don't think so. I mean, it tells us about the key finding – what you found, in what organisms, under what conditions – it's probably the best of the lot. It really does encapsulate what the content is … yes, it's the best.

Mya: So maybe it's a good idea to write out what the key finding is and then use that to form the title?

Svenja: Yes, often you'll then just need to use more nouns … to make it more like a title and less like a sentence.

▬▬ 10.1

Milan: Good afternoon, everybody. I'd like to start by thanking you all for coming to my talk today. My name is Milan Poborski and I'm a PhD candidate at Northumbria University. I'm going to talk today about my recent research investigating the possibility of detecting the secretion of the cytokine MIG, or CXCL9, as a way to measure vaccine-induced T-cell responses. The research was done in the context of a phase 1 vaccine trial of a recombinant viral vector vaccine. To start with, I'll explain briefly how T-cell responses have generally been assessed and outline some of the reasons why this method is imperfect. After that, I'll describe the alternative method I have been investigating, and present the results I have obtained using this method. Finally, I will discuss why this method could be useful as a way to measure vaccine-induced T-cell responses. I plan to talk for about 40 minutes, leaving plenty of time for questions at the end of my talk.

▬▬ 10.2

1 A number of potential vaccine types have been developed and I will be returning to those shortly.

2 As I have already said, counting interferon-gamma secreting cells has been the preferred method to date.

3 As you can see from this image, using flow cytometry to detect MIG secretion gives a more accurate way of measuring immune responses.

4 Let's begin by looking at the size of the malaria problem. Malaria kills over one million people every year in 109 countries.

5 That's all I have to say about the vaccine itself, so now I'd like to move on to looking at judging the response of the immune system to the vaccine.

10.3

1 As I mentioned earlier, there are a number of different vaccine types, but the one I have been working with is an attenuated viral vaccine developed by the …

2 The immune response to the vaccine has been measured using the *ex vivo* interferon-gamma ELISPOT, which has had some problems, and I'll deal with this point later.

3 We've looked at the methodology used, so now let's turn to the results.

4 In fact, the charts here indicate that detecting MIG by flow cytometry and RT-PCR is actually more sensitive than detecting interferon-gamma with these methods.

5 Next we'll look at the potential application of this alternative method.

10.4

Milan: So let me recap what I've said. Many methods are currently being investigated to measure the immune response to the malaria vaccines under development. Using MIG as a marker has the potential to increase sensitivity, without needing to increase the volume of blood needed. I therefore believe that intracellular staining for MIG could be used alongside current methods to detect vaccine-induced T cells. That brings me to the end of my talk today. I would like to thank you for being such an attentive audience and I would be happy to answer any questions you may have. Thank you.

10.5

Conversation 1

Milan: And which session did you say you'd just been to?

Mosi: I don't think I did! I went to Zak Meyer's paper on blood-stage vaccines.

Milan: Ah, yes. The abstract for that one looked interesting. How was it?

Mosi: Well, to be honest it was a bit too clinical for me. I thought it was going to be about vaccine development.

Milan: Oh, and it wasn't? That's what I thought from the abstract …

Conversation 2

Milan: Sorry … erm, excuse me, do you mind if I join you?

Freja: No, no, not at all.

Jacob: Jacob Sachs.

Milan: I'm Milan Poborski.

Jacob: And this is Freja Pedersen.

Milan: Nice to meet you, Freja.

Conversation 3

Milan: So where are you based, Freja?

Freja: Oh, I was at UF with Jacob, but I'm at UND now.

Milan: Ah, right. And what are you working on? Parasitology, right?

Freja: Yeah, that's right. And you, Milan? What are you looking at?

Conversation 4

Freja: Milan, do you know Makareta? She used to do parasitology at UND, too.

Milan: No. Hi.

Makareta: Nice to meet you, Milan.

Milan: So are you giving a paper here, Makareta?

Makareta: Oh, well, I gave it yesterday … late in the afternoon, unfortunately.

Conversation 5

Milan: So Makareta, have you been to Cambridge before?

Makareta: No, it's my first time. It seems nice though. Not that I've been out much.

Milan: Well, how about you come out with us tonight? A group of us are going to go to a restaurant.

Makareta: Yeah, that sounds good. Look, sorry, Milan, but I have to go. I said I'd meet a friend to help her practise her talk. I'll see you later on though.

Conversation 6

Milan: Freja! I've been looking for you. So, how did the talk go? Did you get a good turnout?

Freja: Yes, it was fine. I was so nervous, though! But I had quite a few people – not too many – and I got some really good questions, so that was helpful. And I can relax and enjoy the rest of the conference now.

Conversation 7

Makareta: So which other sessions have you been to today, Milan?

Milan: Oh, well, I didn't go to anything this morning, because I wanted to have a final practice before I did mine.

Makareta: Fair enough.

Milan: But this afternoon, after I'd been to support Mosi with his poster, I went to a couple on vaccine development. One was by Joan Cummings …

Conversation 8

Milan: It's good to finally meet you, Jacob, and put a face to the name. I've just been reading a lot of your lab's work on TNF receptors and malaria protection.

Jacob: Ah, excellent. And you said you were at Northumbria, Milan? Do you work with Percy Grey?

Milan: Yes, that's right. Erm, Jacob, this might seem a little forward, but I wondered what opportunities there were in your lab for post-doctoral positions … I mean, I'll be handing in soon, so hopefully …

10.6

1 Excuse me for interrupting. I really enjoyed your talk.

2 Oh, I've just noticed the time. Good luck tomorrow.

3 Nice talking to you. I'll see you around.

4 I want to talk to you.

5 I'm going now.

6 Sorry to interrupt.

7 I'd better go and find my colleague.

8 I'm Jose-Luis. What's your name?

10.7

Participant: Hi, excuse me. Yes, um, I was just wondering, could you tell me a bit about your work here?

Mosi: Oh, hello, yes of course, well, we know that viral-based malaria vaccines could contribute to the prevention of the disease and most studies so far have focused on describing antigen-specific T-cell responses to these vaccines. My research though focuses on changes in Natural Killer cell populations which may act directly as anti-malarials, or could be influencing the T-cell responses. In this study, human volunteers, who had not had malaria, were vaccinated with a viral-based vaccine, and then the T-cell and NK-cell responses were measured. As you can see in this chart, numbers of CD56[bright] lymphocytes increased significantly following vaccination, while the number of CD56[dim] cells did not increase. The second graph shows that there was no significant correlation between the CD56 populations and the antigen-specific T-cell responses. It seems then that measuring antigen-specific T cells is more meaningful than NK cells as an indicator of immune response in these vaccination regimens.

Participant: Interesting, interesting. Just one thing though. Could you just clarify how the NK cells …

10.8

A

Mosi: The important difference here is the way the two cell types contribute to the immune response. As I was just mentioning to the gentleman here, CD56[bright] cells produce a range of cytokines which stimulate other cells. They are not killers themselves. The CD56[dim] cells, however, are cytotoxic, so they are actually killer cells. Is that what you wanted to know about them?

B

Mosi: Yes, of course. The T-cell responses were measured using *ex vivo* ELISPOT. The NK-cell population was determined by flow cytometry and intracellular staining. If you want to know more about the specifics of the protocol or the reagents I used, just send me an email. The address is here, on this handout and on my card.

C

Mosi: Sure. So I mentioned two kinds of NK cells; those which are CD56[bright] and those which are CD56[dim]. The bright kind don't actually kill, despite the name. What they do is secrete cytokines like interferon-gamma which can then stimulate the helper T cells. Does that answer your question?

ANSWER KEY

Unit 1

2a
- ✔ teaching (undergraduate) students
- ✔ doing post-doctoral research
- ✗ supervising a research team
- ✔ finding a permanent position at a university
- ✔ discussing theory
- ✗ doing practical fieldwork
- ✗ staying in London
- ✗ finding a well-paid job

b/c
likes or dislikes: Sentences 3 and 5
past experiences: Sentences 2 and 7
future (more certain): Sentences 1 and 6
future (possible): Sentences 4 and 8

4a
1 No – the scholarship is for the individual, not for an organisation.
2 Student's own answers
3 Personal details – name, address, education/qualifications, research experience
Project proposal – what you want to work on, where and with whom; how much funding you will need; why it is useful research
4 These potential leaders will be able to guide future research and train and mentor future researchers. The investment in one leader now will therefore be amplified in the future.

b
1 j   2 e   3 i   4 c   5 h
6 g   7 b   8 a   9 d   10 f

5b
Possible applications for the robot technology could include many of the functions sniffer dogs are used for today, for example:
- in rescue operations following disasters (earthquakes, avalanches etc.) to detect bodies
- to detect chemical/gas leaks (e.g. in mining)
- at customs to detect plant matter, drugs and other materials
- to locate mines or unexploded bombs
- to find truffles

c
A 2   B 6   C 3   D 1   E 5   F 4

d
Suggested answers
B The proposed research will concentrate on …
C This technology will …
D This research aims to …
E This will then (be tested experimentally)
F This should produce …

6a
1 However
2 The proposed research
3 will indicate
4 aims to
5 The study
6 The initial phase

7b
Suggested answer
Computer skills: What programs, applications, programming languages you are familiar with and how proficient you are at using them
Dissertations: The title, a short description of the work and your conclusions, the name(s) of your supervisor(s) and the date it will be finished if in progress
Education: Begin with your most recent or expected degree. List degrees, majors, institutions, and dates of completion (or expected date) in reverse chronological order. You could also list key units.
Grants and awards: Details of any grants or awards you have received – who they were from and for how much money
Personal information: Name, address, telephone number and email address
Presentations: List items in standard bibliographic format
Publications: As presentations, list in standard bibliographic format. Those in press or submitted manuscripts can be included.
Research experience: Job title, the name of the employer or institution, dates, your responsibilities and accomplishments
Study abroad: Where and when you studied, who your supervisors were, what you investigated, what courses you took
Teaching experience: What courses you taught (and in what capacity, e.g. lecturer/tutor), the name of the employer or institution, dates, your responsibilities and accomplishments
Technical skills: Include any additional technical skills you have which will not be immediately obvious from the dissertations/work experience you listed
Travel: Where you have been and why (to work as a volunteer, for pleasure, on business)

8a
1 Education
2 Teaching Experience
3 Grants
4 Awards

c
1 Use a lot of different headings
2 Write the most recent thing first

9a
Yes – he should write his most recent educational experiences first.

b
1 A verb in the past simple. Regular verbs add -(e)d to the root of the word (e.g. produce > produced).
2 It is better first to state what you did and then say why you did it.

c
Suggested answers
1 used pure cloned enzymes to generate specific carbohydrate oligomers
2 created a new CD4 positive HeLa cell clone
3 developed sensitive methods to determine the fine structure of pectins in maize
4 investigated the way the myocardium adapts at the sub-cellular level following exercise

10a
1 1 author's name   2 year
   3 title of article   4 journal name
   5 journal volume and/or issue number
   6 page numbers
2 In press
3 Submitted manuscript

b
1 Hernandez Sanchez, R. and Alvarez, C.M. (2011) 'Salinity and intra-annual variability of perilagoonal vegetation' *Submitted manuscript.*
2 Hernandez Sanchez, R., Gomez Herrera, S.A. and Alvarez, C.M. (2011) 'Declining peri-dunal variability in Doñana' Environmental Management Review. *In press.*
3 Hernandez Sanchez, R. and Alvarez, C.M. (2010) 'Hydroperiod effects on peri-dunal vegetation' Spanish Hydrology Journal Vol 2. pp167–184

12
1 By conference call
2 Confirm her availability for the date and time, upload a video of her presenting her research proposal

3 **Suggested answer**

She cannot see the interviewers, there might be a time delay between UK/Australia, it might be difficult to hear what is said

13b

2 He says she speaks too quickly.

d

1 clearly
2 louder
3 stronger
4 pause
5 problem
6 English
7 speaker

e

1 Yes
2 Yes

f

2 research (NB: Eriko uses the American English pronunciation. British English would stress this word as 'research')
3 useful
4 example
5 However, number, problems

14a

1 see
2 phone number
3 application form
4 questions
5 late
6 tone of voice
7 shuffle
8 comfortable position
9 facing
10 thank

▬▬ Unit 2

1a

1 f   2 a   3 b   4 e   5 d   6 c

c

Suggested answers

a because developments in one specialism within the field can contribute to research in other areas; to network; to ensure they have a more rounded picture of the field; for general interest
b to share protocols/materials/results; to compare findings; to network; to 'bounce' ideas off one another; to avoid replication of experiments; to collaborate on particular areas of research
c for general interest; because the boundaries between fields are often blurred; because developments in one field can have a knock-on effect on other fields

d

Suggested answers

1 A popular science magazine or book. Maybe a newspaper.
2 A conference; An online forum
3 An online forum; An academic journal; A conference

2a

A 6 (a popular science magazine) or 2 (an online forum or science blog)
B 3 or 6 (a newspaper or a popular science magazine)
C 4 (an academic journal) or possibly 6 (a popular science magazine)
D 2 (an online forum or science blog)
E 4 (an academic journal)
Not included 1 (a conference), 5 (a popular science book)

3a

1 does anyone know …?
2 be down to
3 :–(, Thanks!
4 say researchers in *Archives of Internal Medicine*
5 Lipton *et al.* (2010)
6 This was a prospective observational study
7 will need to be verified
8 *in vitro*

b

Features 5,6,7 and 8 are appropriate for formal scientific research papers
Features 1,2, 3, and 4 are appropriate for personal communication

4c

Post A: a 1, b 2, c 3
Post B: a 2, b 1, c 3
Post C: a 3, b 1, 2

d

There is no question word, no articles (*a, an, the*) and no main verb (can't in B belongs to the relative clause *which can't …*; *considered* in C is a past participle)

5

Suggested answers

2 If you use an inappropriate style, your work will not be respected and it may not even be understood. Even good research may not be published if written in an inappropriate style.
3 Every time you look at a text in English, keep a record of <u>where</u> you read it (a book, a text message, a research paper), <u>why</u> it was written (to entertain, to arrange a meeting, to report new research), <u>who</u> it was written for (the public, a friend, the scientific community), then underline useful words and phrases that you only/mostly find used in those texts.

6a

Suggested answers

2 The science reported in the media is often exaggerated so, for example, something that was found to reduce stress may be portrayed as curing it, something which causes a small change may be suggested to cause a large change. In addition, the context of the research is often removed or the findings are extrapolated, so a finding in mice for example is presented as applying to humans, a finding in certain people presented as applying to the population as a whole. The difference occurs because bold statements are much more eye-catching and the public is often not (believed to be) interested in details.
3 You could look at the report of the same research in a science magazine or, even better, look at the original journal article.

b

Suggested answers

a If you read research *critically*, it means that you think about what you are reading, considering what is good and what is not good about the research used (particularly the method used and the conclusions drawn from the results).
b You should always read research critically because it allows you to judge how reliable the results obtained are and how credible the conclusions drawn are.

7a

1 Two (*a couple of*) paragraphs: a brief summary and then Ryuchi's opinion
2 No, Ryuchi needs to read the whole paper in order to write a critical review of it.
3 Read the abstract first, make a table and note the key points from each section of the paper.
4 Yes
5 Ryuchi should make his own notes (it will help him write the review in his own words).

b

Introduction: 4, 7
Method: 1, 5, 6
Results: 3
Discussion: 2

d

The questions which can be answered are:

Method

1 *What variables were investigated?* Changes in cortisol and catecholamines in urine, and changes in energy metabolism and in gut microbial activities before eating

dark chocolate and after 8 and 15 days of eating 40 g chocolate/day in high and low anxiety participants

5 *Who/What was studied?* 30 young healthy adults

6 *What procedure was used?* Questionnaire to divide group into high vs low anxiety; Blood and urine samples taken; 40 g chocolate/day given for 14 days; Blood and urine samples taken again at 8 days and 15 days

Results

3 *What were the main findings?* All participants had lower levels of stress hormones in the blood; the high and low anxiety groups had more similar energy metabolism and gut microbial activity after eating the chocolate than before.

Discussion

2 *How did the authors interpret the results?* 40 g chocolate a day for 2 weeks can change metabolism. This could affect health in the long term.

e

1 short
2 reduces
3 stress
4 anxiety
5 control
6 chocolate
7 same
8 placebo
9 metabolic
10 blind

8a

1 No, they don't include all the main points from the notes. Not mentioned are:

From the summary column:
– The researcher's interpretations of the results as presented in the discussion section of the table

From the opinion column:
– The short trial period
– The fact that they did not look at stress levels / reported anxiety after eating the chocolate
– The suggestions for improving the study (i.e. need more people with the same anxiety levels / give chocolate or placebo / look at long-term changes / use a blind trial)

2 a Extract A summarises part of the research
  b Extract B gives an evaluation

b

a One problem with this research is; In addition / Furthermore
b Furthermore / In addition
c changes in [blood flow] were analysed
d The research found
e The results cannot be applied to; making it impossible to
f Blood samples were taken

c

A paragraph which summarises the research: f, b, c, d
A paragraph which gives an evaluation: a, e

10a

1 To remind members of staff that protecting their work and using their work commercially are important

b

1 D   2 C   3 B   4 E   5 A

c

Suggested answers

2 MTAs may be needed for things like:
  • substances (e.g. chemical, pharmaceutical, nucleic acid)
  • biological organisms (e.g. virus, bacteria, cells, animals, plants)
  • genetically modified organisms (e.g. animal, plant, micro-organism)
  • biological materials (e.g. tissues, blood, urine or other body products)
  • software
  • nuclear materials
Any material that is commercially available will not require an MTA.

3 Details of who the individuals/ organisations involved are; what the material is and what it is to be used for; where the material will be used/stored; whether approval has been given for its use (e.g. biosafety approval / ethics approval); whether it will be used for commercial gain

11b

1 No   2 No   3 Yes   4 Yes
5 No   6 Yes   7 Joint   8 Yes

c

Suggested answers

1 A lay summary is a summary written for the general public, not for an expert in the field. Anyone should be able to understand it.

2 He should avoid very technical language or jargon although some amount of detail will be needed. He should keep the writing impersonal, for example by avoiding personal pronouns and by using passive forms. He should avoid exclamation marks, emoticons, etc.

3 The reader may be an administrator rather than a scientist. If they are a scientist, they will not necessarily work in Binh's field.

4 A lay summary is required so that whoever reads it can understand it – no specific knowledge is necessary.

d

1 material is samples of
2 different types of

3 will be stained to show
4 The aim of the research is to investigate

1a

1 termite mound
2 snail shell
3 boxfish
4 mosquito
5 beetle
6 plant leaves

b

1 **Suggested answers**
  • bacterial control inspired by red algae
  • vaccines without refrigeration inspired by resurrection plant
  • fibre manufacture inspired by golden orb weaver spiders
  • water purification inspired by the marsh ecosystem
  • pacemaker replacement inspired by humpback whales
  • fire retardant inspired by animal cells
  • self-assembling glass inspired by sea sponges
  • wound healing inspired by flies
  • optical brighteners inspired by *Cyphochilus* beetle

2 More or less any science discipline can be included in a biomimetics group depending on what they are trying to mimic.

2b

1 Only the parts of the surface which face the spray can be covered.
2 By dipping the implant in a saturated solution and encouraging the coating to 'grow'.

3a

1 To find out where the 'gap' is; to check what you are thinking of doing has not been done before; to get ideas about possible methodologies

2 By searching a database for key terms; by asking others in your area for ideas of what to read; by reading a review and then looking at the sources cited

3 Plan her research; write a review

b

1 D   2 B, E   3 A, C

c

1 follow-up study (Extract E)
2 application(s) (Extract D)
3 irregular (Extract C)
4 induce(d) (Extract A)
5 modify(ing) (Extract D)
6 maintain(ing) (Extract D)
7 decompose(d) (Extract A)
8 enhance (Extract E)

e
1 Yes
2 No. She has changed words (paraphrased)
3 By citing the sources (author + date)
4 'And others'. Used when there are more than two authors

f
a However
b In addition

g
1 In contrast   2 Moreover
3 On the other hand   4 Therefore
5 As a result

h
- Studies have found better survival rates for coated implants (Havelin *et al.*, 2000), but the usual plasma-spray technique cannot coat all surfaces evenly (Pilliar, 2005).
- However, the usual plasma-spray technique cannot coat all surfaces evenly (Pilliar, 2005) and the plasma-spraying process causes CaP input powders to break down into other compounds such as tetra calcium phosphate (Radin and Ducheyne, 1992).

i
Suggested answer
All four ways are possible, but version (b) is probably the best.
In version (a) the sentences may be too short.
Version (b) is in an appropriate style and presents the information in a logical order by combining the two facts about the spraying process in one sentence and information about the survival rate in another.
Version (c) is in an appropriate style and emphasises the important contrast between (Sentence 2) and (Sentence 3). However, the sentences in (b) are in a more logical grouping.
Version (d) may be too long for a single sentence.

j
1 First   2 so   3 However
4 and   5 In addition

4b
1 A (super-)hydrophilic material is one which attracts water; a (super-)hydrophobic material is one which repels water
2 A water-harvesting material
3 The Namib desert beetle's wings
4 She plans to develop a superhydrophobic material which has a surface covered in superhydrophilic bumps

c   Suggested answer

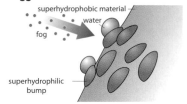

superhydrophobic material
water
fog
superhydrophilic bump

d
Yes, he is (at the end of the conversation after Rayna describes the commercial application of her design).

e
1 Because it *seems to double the work*. Rayna's idea needs two surfaces (hydrophilic and hydrophobic), whereas the lotus design needs only one (a hydrophobic surface).
2 Because Rayna's material could *collect water just from fog, not raindrops, so you wouldn't need actual rainfall*
3 Rayna thinks that *nets must be less efficient because of the holes in them*. A solid material would stop more fog.
4 To collect water for drinking etc. in refugee camps; to collect and recycle water in cooling towers in factories
5 The use in cooling towers as it *sounds like a profitable use*

5a
1 Because of   2 Because
3 because   4 so   5 because of

c
The version from audioscript 3.2 is more polite because it uses phrases that are less certain and less direct (*I think ... could be ... might be ...*). This shows that the speaker is more modest.

d
Suggested answer
1 I think that biomimetic solar panels which move with the sun **could** be created by using alternative materials and designs.
2 They **would** be useful in developing areas, where motor-based sun-tracking panels are not affordable.
3 Also, **it seems to me that** solar cells that track the sun **would** probably **be** more efficient at generating power than those in a fixed position.

7b
1 Sahal: hard to listen to many people; topic changed quickly so he became confused
2 Hitomi: everyone talked at the same time; she couldn't find a way to join in

3 Sam: couldn't concentrate for such a long time; he missed important questions; he was asked a question but couldn't answer
4 Radek: didn't know how to interrupt, ask questions, etc., politely

8a
1 The structure of many ridges, covered by millions of setae ending in hundreds of spatulae, increases the surface area which can come into contact, and so form attractive forces, with the surface.
2 By aligning the setae so the spatulae are flat against the surface and then sliding the foot to create shear force, the gecko can stick.
3 By changing the shape of the setae to increase the angle with the surface, the forces are reduced and the foot can peel away.
4 So few spatulae stick to the piece of dirt that the forces between the dirt and the surface are larger than those between the foot and the dirt, hence the dirt is 'pulled off' the foot.

b
1 He's been using a curved setal model rather than the usual straight ones.
2 He asks why Deepak has been focusing on forces in one single seta.

c
Students will have their own opinion on this. Answer to be revealed later.

d
No, he isn't. He seems to be trying to clarify his question. He says things like 'No, I've got that', and 'No, I know what they are ...' to show that Deepak isn't answering his question.

e
1 It was relevant.
2 Yes, he thinks it was relevant and acknowledges the 'gap' in the research and the need for another collaborator.

9a
In some countries and cultures, it is not appropriate for a junior scientist to interrupt and/or be critical of a senior colleague's ideas. However, it is often more acceptable in an English-speaking scientific culture (if done politely and constructively).

b
Sorry, Sarah. Could I just ask what kind of forces?
Erm, sorry. Can I just check I understood?
Sorry, could you quickly explain that? I'm not quite sure what you mean.
Erm, could I jump in and ask a question?

10a
1 Well
2 So
3 Right
4 Anyway
5 Erm

b
They all signal the start of a turn.
That is, they show that someone in
the conversation would like to say
something.

Unit 4

1a
- analyse data
- collect data
- conduct (or run) an experiment
- define the question
- design an experiment
- draw conclusions
- form a hypothesis
- interpret data

b
1 define the question
2 form a hypothesis
3 design an experiment
4 conduct (or run) an experiment
5 collect data
6 analyse data
7 interpret data
8 draw conclusions

d
analyse – analysis
collect – collection
design – design (*this word uses the same form for the verb and the noun*)
explain – explanation
form – formation
observe – observation
relate – relationship
run – run (*this word uses the same form for the verb and the noun*)
vary – variable

2a
1 Theoretical   2 Field   3 Internal
4 Descriptive   5 Quantitative

b
Suggested answers
1 Practical research: A linear
accelerator was used to accelerate
electrons up to 20 GeV. Due to
the high energy and momentum
of the electron it is able to probe
inside the proton. As the energy
of the electron increased, there
was far more scattering at larger
angles than expected. This suggests
the proton is not an elementary
(fundamental) particle but is made
of smaller, point-like particles which
could deflect the electron by a large
amount.

2 Laboratory experiment: To examine
precipitation and temperature
effects on populations of *Aedes
albopictus*, caged populations of
the mosquito were maintained at
22, 26, and 30 °C. All cages were
assigned to one of three simulated
precipitation treatment regimes.
3 External validity: To investigate the
link between economic status and
likelihood of smoking in 18–25
year-old males, survey questionnaires
were sent out to students picked
at random from the university's
database.
4 Experimental study: The effects
of eating soy on breast cancer
incidence were investigated. Half
of the subjects ate at least one
soy-based product a day, while the
second group, the control group,
ate an essentially soy-free diet.
During the 30 years of the study, the
women's incidence of breast cancer
was recorded.
5 Qualitative research: To investigate
the effect of eating dark chocolate
on stress levels, subjects completed
a questionnaire rating their stress
levels. After eating the chocolate, the
questionnaire was filled in again.

3a
1 Hydrogen is environmentally friendly,
renewable and easily produced from
water.
2 Hydrogen can be used in any
application in which fossil fuels
(i.e. coal, petroleum and natural
gas) are being used today, with the
exception of cases in which carbon is
specifically needed. Hydrogen can be
used as a fuel in furnaces, internal
combustion engines, turbines and
jet engines and is more efficient than
fossil fuels. Cars, buses, trains, ships,
submarines, aeroplanes and rockets
can run on hydrogen. Hydrogen
can also be converted directly to
electricity by fuel cells, with a variety
of applications in transportation and
stationary power generation.

b Suggested answers
a **Advantages:** it would be easier to fill
a car, etc. with gas than with liquid
hydrogen
Disadvantages: needs a large
tank and high pressures to store;
high pressure difficult to contain
safely; tank would need to be very
heavy in order to counteract the lift
generated by the hydrogen
b **Advantages:** tank lighter than for
gas storage

Disadvantages: large amount of
energy needed to cool hydrogen
enough to liquefy it; tanks must be
well insulated to keep cold; liquid
hydrogen has a low energy density
by volume
c **Advantages:** carbon is a possible
porous material – high availability
and low cost; takes little space to
store; safe
Disadvantages: high pressures and/
or low temperatures needed for
hydrogen adsorption; material may
not release the hydrogen easily

c
1 adsorbed onto a porous material
2 porosity (of the carbon fibres)
3 They discuss five different variables:
carbonisation temperature; type of
hydroxide (potassium or sodium);
ratio of hydroxide to carbon fibres;
heating rate; nitrogen flow rate
4 look at the papers mentioned, see
what they found to be the optimal
conditions, and start by replicating
those

d
✔ carbonisation temperature
✔ type of hydroxide (potassium or
sodium)
✔ ratio of KOH or NaOH to carbon
fibres

e
The results will become too difficult
to analyse. It might be difficult to
reproduce (*replicate*) the data.

f
1 affects   2 collecting   3 data
4 dependent   5 independent
6 controlled

g
1 **Controlled:** nitrogen flow rate;
heating rate; carbonisation
temperature; ratio of hydroxide to
carbon fibres
Independent: type of hydroxide
2 **Dependent variable:** hydrogen
adsorption

4a
1 the future
2 suggestions
3 adverbs (*maybe/perhaps*) and modal
verbs (*could/should/might/will*)
4 an infinitive verb (without *to*)

b
Suggested discussion points
Use a laboratory experiment to do
practical research. Ensure internal
validity by changing only one variable
– everything else must be the same
between groups. The study should be
experimental and quantitative.

Caged populations of the mosquito should be used. The cage size and number of mosquitoes in each cage should be identical. To measure the effects of temperature, cages are maintained at different temperatures (e.g. 22, 26, and 30 °C) for an identical length of time. To measure the effect of rainfall, different rainfall regimes should be simulated. The study should be done in such a way that each different rainfall regime is examined at each different temperature. The number of mosquitoes at the end of the treatment period is then counted.

5a
1 b   2 e   3 f   4 c   5 h   6 d
7 g   8 a

b
-graph   shows that the instrument writes, draws or records
-meter   shows that the instrument measures a unit of something
-scope   shows that the instrument is used to see something

c
pH – litmus paper
radiation – geiger counter
changes in voltage over time – oscilloscope
light intensity – spectrometer
distance – calipers
torque – dynamometer
motion – seismograph
wavelengths of light – interferometer

6a/b
a   activation
b   weight
c   ceramic/steel
d   steel/ceramic
e   furnace
f   temperature
g   cooling
h   nitrogen

7a
1 e   2 b   3 g   4 a   5 f   6 c
7 d

b
1   More confident: I'm going to, I'm planning to, I'll try
    More tentative: I was thinking of, I think I'll try, I thought I should, I was planning on
2   INFINITIVE: I'm going to, I thought I should, I'm planning to
    VERB-ing: I was thinking of, I think I'll try, I'll try, I was planning on

8a
1 steel   2 quartz   3 1.5 / 6–7.5
4 75

b
1 were   2 don't   3 would   4 think

The sentences are used to make suggestions.

10a

noun	verb	adjective
compression	compress	compressed
adsorption/ adsorbent	adsorb	adsorbent
activation	activate	activated
porosity		porous

b
1   -sion/-tion e.g. concentration, equation, diffraction
    -ent e.g. referent, detergent, solvent
    -ity e.g. electricity, activity, flexibility
2   -ed e.g. dissolved, used, electrified
    -ent e.g. different, luminescent, fluent
    -ous e.g. bulbous, contagious, fibrous
3   As part of guessing the meaning of new words from the context; to help select the right part of speech when writing

c
1   brittleness
2   capacitance
3   concentration
4   conductivity
5   density
6   flammability
7   luminance
8   mass
9   permeability
10 porosity
11 pressure
12 reactivity
13 solubility
14 velocity
15 viscosity
16 volume

d
1 aluminium   2 glass   3 neon
4 oxygen   5 ethanol   6 blood

e
noun suffixes: -ance; -bility; -ity; -ness; -osity; -tion
adjective suffixes: -able; -ent (more common as an adjective than as a noun); -ive; -ous

f
1   F – To concentrate a solution, add more solute. To dilute it, add more solvent.
2   T
3   T
4   T

g
concentrate – concentration
conduct – conductivity
dissolve – solubility
permeate – permeability

h
1 extract   2 absorb   3 malleability
4 reflectivity   5 detectable

12a
the type of hydroxide

b
1 If   2 will probably   3 more
4 expect   5 any   6 between
7 My prediction is that   8 lead to
9 allow

13a
1   If the fibres are more porous
2   they adsorb more hydrogen
3   Fibres adsorb more hydrogen if they are more porous.

b
1   a   Sentence (a) expresses something you know to be true – the result is not in doubt; sentence (b) expresses what you are fairly sure the result will be.
    b   Sentence (b) expresses what you are fairly sure the result will be; sentence (c) expresses what you think the result will be, although you are less sure than in (b).
    c   Sentence (b) expresses what you are fairly sure the result will be; sentence (d) expresses a less likely result, although still possible.
2   No, the tense in the if-clause remains the same.

14
What should happen is:
1   There is no change to the time for the pendulum swing.
2   There is no change to the time for the pendulum swing.
3   The time gets shorter as the string gets shorter.

Unit 5

1
3   **Suggested answer**
    If you are describing an experimental process in a paper or poster, you need to include sufficient detail that another scientist could replicate your method. This means you need to include details like what you did, under what conditions, using what equipment or reagents, for what timings.

2a
1   The Earth has four major layers: the inner core, outer core, mantle and crust. The crust and the top of the mantle make up a thin layer on the surface of the Earth, but rather than being continuous, this layer is made up of a number of pieces, called tectonic plates, which

fit together like a jigsaw puzzle. These pieces are always moving around, sliding past one another and bumping into each other. Since the edges of the plates are rough, they sometimes get stuck against each other. While the edges of faults are stuck together, the rest of the block is moving. The energy that would normally cause the blocks to slide past one another is being stored up. Eventually the force of the moving blocks builds up so that the friction of the rough edges of the fault is no longer enough to stop the plates from moving. The blocks suddenly move, releasing all the stored-up energy. This is an earthquake.

2 As the plates rub against each other, pressure and temperature build up. If the minerals in the mantle stay strong at high temperatures and pressures, it will take longer for the temperature and pressure to build up enough for an earthquake to occur. However, if they lose strength at lower temperatures and pressures, earthquakes will occur more easily.

c
A powdered mineral sample
B tube of rolled rhenium
C ceramic octahedron
D two tungsten-rhenium thermocouple leads
E tungsten carbide cubes
F six secondary anvils in the press

3a
Multi-anvil high pressure apparatus **was used** to generate the high pressure and temperature for the specimen. The powdered mineral sample **was placed** into a tube of rolled rhenium. The rhenium tube **was loaded** into a ceramic octahedron. Two tungsten-rhenium thermocouple leads **were attached** to the octahedron. The octahedron **was surrounded** by a set of eight tungsten carbide cubes. The cubes **were placed** into the space formed by six secondary anvils in the press. The press **was pumped up** to the correct pressure. The anvils **transform** the directed force of the hydraulic press to hydrostatic pressure on the sample. Heating of the tube **was carried out** using an electrical current conducted through the anvils. Temperature **was controlled** with a programmable temperature controller. Energy diffraction patterns **were collected** using a germanium solid state detector. The patterns **were analysed** to work out the material's strength.
1 past simple passive
2 *was/were* + past participle

3 The passive is used to suggest that anyone who follows the same scientific procedure will get the same results. The passive is used when the person who did the action is less important than the process the verb describes.
4 *transform*. The anvil is an important part of the procedure. In this case, it is important what does the action so we use it as the subject.

b
place into, load into, attach to, surround by, form by, pump up to, carry out, conduct through, control with, work out

c
1 b 2 a 3 b 4 a 5 c 6 a

4b
● use linking words, to make the stages clear (but not too many)
● combine sentences

c
First, the powdered mineral sample was placed into a tube of rolled rhenium, **which** was **then** loaded into a ceramic octahedron.

d
The rhenium tube in the second sentence is replaced with *which*.

e
● Two tungsten-rhenium thermocouple leads were attached to the octahedron, which was then surrounded by a set of eight tungsten carbide cubes.
● The cubes were placed into the space formed by six secondary anvils in the press, which was then pumped up to the correct pressure.

5a
1 First 2 was 3 which 4 then
5 at   6 which

6b
differential stress the difference between the greatest and the least compressive stress experienced by an object.
stress a measurement of the average force on a surface
yield to change shape because of the force on an object
yield strength the amount of stress which can be put on an object before it deforms (changes shape)

c
● differential stress in the olivine and perovskite samples will go up with pressure ✔
● perovskite will be stronger than olivine, i.e. it will yield later ✔
● for olivine, increasing the temperature will reduce yield strength ✔

● for perovskite, increasing the temperature will reduce yield strength ✘

d
1 increase temperature; increase pressure
2 that the results are accurate

7a
1 that; would; did
2 as
3 that; would
4 did
5 thought; would

b
Expectations: I thought that the differential stress in all of the samples would go up; I expected that increasing the temperature would reduce; I thought the minerals would all be affected
Outcomes: it did; as I expected; that's what did happen
1 To show that these are past expectations. We often use *will* for present expectations (e.g. *I **think** that the differential stress in the sample **will** go up*), so to talk about past expectations *will* changes to *would*.
2 *did* emphasises the fact that his prediction was correct.

8a
● To date → so far
● have been investigated → I've looked at
● In addition, some research has been carried out → I've also done a couple of runs
● increased with pressure → go up as the pressure increased, and it did.
● has the highest strength → was the strongest
● decreases significantly → went right down
● increases → went up

b
There is a difference in the level of formality between the spoken and written forms. The spoken version is less formal.

c
1 **In addition**, petrography studies have been **carried out**.
2 Sodic glasses contained **the highest** number of cations with low average field strength and non-sodic glasses the lowest.
3 In all five tephra samples, Al_2O_3 decreased **with** the increase in SiO_2.
4 **To date**, the morphology and mineralogy of tephra samples from La Malinche **have been** examined.

11a/b
1 The samples might not be ringwoodite at all. (unlikely)
2 The machine might need to be recalibrated. (possible)

12a
1 a   2 b   3 c   4 c   5 b

13a
1 surprising
2 similar
3 appears
4 possible
5 possibly
6 unlikely
7 possibility
8 likely

b
a Because of
b As a result,
c However,
d Firstly,
e Although
f Therefore,

15a/b
1 d   2 i   3 h   4 k   5 b   6 c
7 j   8 g   9 f   10 e   11 l   12 a

c
Suggested answers
1 ↓
2 °C
3 K (NB: the ° is not used with K)
4 ≥
5 +
6 v/v
7 w/o
8 2:1
9 h
10 conc.

e
1 RT
2 378 K
3 Δ
4 K
5 ↓
6 7
7 conc.

16b
1 share
2 notes
3 search
4 changes
5 group's
6 safer

17a
a 3   b 5   c 1   d 4   e 2

b

	Past	Present
Ability/ Possibility	*could do*	**can share**
Advice	*should have done*	**should try**
Lack of obligation	*didn't have to do* *didn't need to do*	**don't need to worry**
Obligation	**had to use**	*must do*
Prohibition	**were never allowed to take**	*are not allowed to do* *can't do* *mustn't do*

Unit 6

1a
1 d   2 h   3 a   4 g   5 i   6 f
7 c   8 e   9 b

b
2 nano = 10^{-9}
3 re = again
4 endo = (move) inside
5 over = too much
6 multi = many
7 inter = between
8 en = inside
9 in = in(to)

c
1 Nanotechnology is the area of science which deals with developing and producing nano- (very small) devices, tools and machines.
2 **Suggested answers**
   medicine (diagnosis, tissue engineering, drug delivery)
   chemistry (catalysts, filters)
   energy (increasing efficiency and reducing consumption)
   information/communication (memory storage, semiconductors)
   engineering (aerospace, construction)

2a
a The nanotube surface is functionalised with a chemical receptor and the drug molecules are encapsulated.
b The open end of the tube is capped.
c After the nanocapsule is ingested, it locates to target site due to the functionalised surface.
d The cell internalises the capsule, for example by receptor-mediated endocytosis.
e The cap is removed or biodegrades inside the cell.
f The drug molecules are released.

b
1 F – He asks her to explain what is happening in the diagram.
2 T
3 F – It is sometimes called a 'magic bullet' because it sends the drug to where it is needed.
4 F – Her main interest is in how to encapsulate the drug in a nanotube.
5 T – It can be swallowed, injected or inhaled.
6 T – She uses biodegradable caps.

3a
1 coat; with
2 attach; to
3 in
4 encapsulated
5 internalised; by
6 dissolves

b
1 c   2 a   3 e   4 b   5 d

c
1 diluted
2 ground into
3 purify
4 rinsed with
5 fuse together

4a
1 O   2 A   3 A   4 O   5 O

5a
● There are too many sequencing words; it's better to just write in order and only use words like 'then' when you really need to.
● Don't use 'I' or 'We'; use passives.
● Change 'for target …' to 'to target …' to say why something is done.
● Use present tense (not past) to describe a process in general; use the past tense for specific experiments.
● Take out the sentence with examples of ways to ingest the tubes; never include information the reader doesn't need to understand your work.

b
The magic bullet process uses carbon nanotubes to send a drug to a specific target. **The surface of the nanotubes is functionalised** by coating it with chemical receptors. For example, **to** target a tumour which overexpresses folic acid, folate receptors are attached to its surface. **The drug molecules are encapsulated** within the nanotube. **Then** the tube is capped and the nanotubes are ingested. Once inside the body, the nanotube locates to the target site. **The nanotube is internalised by the target cell** by receptor-mediated endocytosis. After that, the cap is either removed or biodegraded and the drug molecules are released into the cell.

6a

1 The tissue surface was rinsed with ice-cold isotonic saline solution.
2 After incubation at 37 °C for 60 minutes, the suspension was diluted to 100 ml with water.
3 Particles as small as 10 μm are filtered out using a mesh.
4 The audiometric thresholds are measured at six frequencies from 250 Hz to 8 kHz. / The audiometric thresholds at six frequencies from 250 Hz to 8 kHz are measured.
5 Densitometry was used to analyse the autoradiograph.

b

Sentences 3 and 4 describe a process in general; Sentences 1, 2 and 5 report a particular procedure.
The present tense is used when describing a process in general. The past tense is used to report a particular procedure which was carried out in one particular experiment or set of experiments.

c

The following sentences have verbs in the passive:
Exercise 3a – 4 (*is encapsulated*), 5 (*is internalised*)
Exercise 3b – 1 (*was used*), 2 (*is caught*), 5 (*was extracted*)
Exercise 3c – 1 (*were diluted*), 2 (*was ground*), 3 (*could be used*), 4 (*was rinsed*), 5 (*is liberated*)
The following sentences could be made more formal by using the passive:
Exercise 3a – 1 (*the surface of the tube is coated*), 2 (*folate receptors are attached*), 3 (*the drug is encapsulated*), 4 (*a cap is used*), 6 (*biodegradable caps are used*)
The following verbs do not need to be changed because they have non-human subjects:
Exercise 3a – 6 (*The cap dissolves*)
Exercise 3b – 2 (*the gas cools, the water vapour condenses*), 3 (*Devices ... would filter out*), 4 (*Haemotoxylin-Eosin stains*)
Exercise 3c – 5 (*two deuterons fuse together*)

8a

1 a   2 c   3 a   4 b   5 b   6 c
7 b   8 b

b

a ¼
b 15%
c 1.356
d 2,905,740
e 5 x 10^9
f −35
g 10^6
h 10,893
i −57
j 17^5/$_8$
k 0.003
l 5,090,019

c

1 a three quarters   b five eighths
  c four ninths   d ten to the power of seven / ten to the seven
  e ten to the power of minus nine / ten to the minus nine
2 a per cent   b times   c minus
3 A **decimal point (.)** describes parts of a whole number; a **comma (,)** separates hundreds from thousands (1,100), hundreds of thousands (110,000), millions (1,100,000), etc.
1.356 = one point three five six;
1,356 = one thousand, three hundred and fifty-six

9a

1 metre	m	length
2 kilogram	kg	mass
3 second	s	time
4 ampere	A	electric current
5 kelvin	K	thermodynamic temperature
6 candela	cd	luminous intensity
7 mole	mol	amount of substance
8 hertz	Hz	frequency
9 joule	J	energy
10 ohm	Ω	resistance
11 degree Celsius	°C	temperature

c

1 kilo-
2 mega-
3 giga-
4 tera-
5 centi-
6 milli-
7 micro-
8 nano-
9 pico-

d

1 mg
2 pmol
3 Ω
4 A
5 K
6 kJ
7 kHz
8 ns

11a

1 b   2 f   3 g   4 e   5 c   6 a
7 d   8 h

b

1 To check the size of the CNTs and the wall thickness, and that they are consistent
2 She suspends the tubes in a solution and puts a drop onto the slide. When the solution evaporates, the CNTs remain on the slide.
3 By capillary action.

12a

@	at
~	approximately

→	leads to
D	diameter
diam.	diameter
EM	electron microscope
L	length
w/	with
w/v	weight per volume

c

1 50
2 700
3 15
4 2-propanol
5 3
6 glass

13a

1 ranged
2 length
3 to
4 average
5 approximately
6 estimated
7 and
8 actual
9 due
10 suspended
11 placed
12 aid
13 evaporated
14 blending
15 with
16 consisted
17 ratio
18 laden
19 covered
20 filled

b

a passive: estimate, place, prepare, suspend
b active: consist, cover, evaporate, fill, investigate, range

c

1 The change in red blood cells ranged from approximately plus 8% to minus 7.4%.
2 The cells were suspended in an incubation medium and then placed in a flask.
3 The stream sediment samples were soaked in HCl at a 1-to-1 volume ratio.

■ Unit 7

1a

1 e   2 f   3 g   4 b   5 a
6 d   7 c

b

1 a It could help show us how/ why some organisms become genetically isolated from other, similar organisms (evolution)
  b It could help us to understand the possible structures and adaptations of early organisms

c It could give us ideas how and where we might search for life on other planets

2 **Suggested answer**
Enzymes that can be used in industrial processes under extreme physical or chemical conditions. For example, for the removal of hydrogen peroxide in the industrial bleaching (cleaning) in the production of paper and textiles.

c
2 alkali- + pH 9 or above
3 cryo- + temperatures of 15 °C or lower
4 metalo- + metals
5 osmo- + high osmotic pressures
6 radio- + radiation
7 thermo- + temperatures between 60 and 80°C

d
a -tolerant   b -resistant   c -phile

e
1 e   2 f   3 g   4 d   5 c   6 a   7 b

f
1 a hyperthermophile
2 a halophobe
3 a neutrophile
4 a polyextremophile

2a
1 high temperatures and high metal concentrations
2 to go up; to show high levels
3 as the control group; to compare them with the vent species of shrimp
4 (4 types of) (antioxidant) enzymes

b
1 h   2 j   3 a   4 d   5 e
6 g   7 b   8 c   9 f   10 i

c
1 samples
2 mean
3 ANOVA
4 t-tests
5 p-value
6 standard deviation
7 correlation
8 regression analysis

3b
1 approximately sixfold higher than in
2 not significantly different from
3 the lowest
4 No significant differences
5 threefold higher in
6 A significantly higher

c Suggested answers
1 *M. fortunata* exhibited a far higher cytosolic SOD activity than any other species.
2 MT levels in *P. elegans* were slightly less than three times higher than those in *P. varians*.

3 No significant difference was seen in the cytosolic CAT levels in the two coastal shrimp species, or in the two vent species. However, the vent species exhibited higher levels than the coastal species.
4 Levels of GPx in *P. varians* were not significantly different from those in *P. elegans* or in *R. exoculata*. However, levels in *P. elegans* and *R. exoculata* were significantly different from each other.

4a
1 Visuals are used in papers to:
   • present a large amount of information in a small space
   • present complicated findings in a clear and simple way
   • draw attention to the key findings

b
1 f   2 d   3 e   4 b   5 c
6 g   7 a

5a
1 row
2 column
3 line graph
4 point
5 scatter plot
6 x-axis
7 line of best fit
8 bar chart
9 y-axis
10 histogram
11 stacked bar chart
12 key
13 label
14 scale
15 caption
16 pie chart

b
a bar chart / table
b scatter plot
c map
d pie chart / stacked bar chart
e diagram
f histogram / line graph

6a
1 axes
2 included
3 show what the colours mean
4 show standard deviation

7a
1 The normal convention is that captions for tables appear <u>above</u> the table, while captions for figures appear <u>below</u> the figure, unless a particular journal specifies otherwise.
2 An explanation of what is being shown; the object of study; the sample size; the location of the study; the treatment applied, and a summary of the statistics; other information such as an explanation of codes used in the figure (a key)

3 The main problem is often being concise and using appropriate noun phrases rather than full sentences.

b
1 In brackets as *n = 51* (where *n* means the number and *51* is the value)
2 There is no main verb in caption A or the underlined part of caption D. They are noun phrases.
3 No; the original authors and the year they published the work are given in brackets (or parentheses)
4 *compared with* The purpose of the table is to make a comparison between a number of different variables (temperature, pH and various chemical concentrations) in three different environments, one of which is seen as 'standard' (average seawater) and two others which are seen as 'special' (lagoon system and vent field).
5 *under investigation*
6 In brackets and in italics. In brackets because it is additional information, not the main point. In italics because it is the Latin, not the English-language name.
7 a It tells the reader what the visual shows or describes.
   b They give the reader information about the experimental process he/she needs in order to understand the information in the visual.
8 *The data represent*
9 *not statistically different*
10 There is no main verb in the underlined part of the caption. It is a noun phrase. The other parts of the caption have main verbs (*represent* and *are*), so are sentences.

8a
1 Length-frequency of four samples of mussels collected at three different sites of the Lucky Strike area.
2 Copper concentration in the soft and exoskeleton tissues of four shrimp species.
3 Comparison of the physical and chemical characteristics of the hydrothermal fluids at Menez Gwen, Lucky Strike and Rainbow (adapted from Douville *et al.*, 2002).

b
1 Fig. 1
2 *B. azoricus*
3 expressed
4 Values
5 represent
6 (p < 0.05)

c
Add brackets to: (cytosolic and mitochondrial), (0.4 μM), and (n=10)

9

1 The text highlights the key results. A chart might show a few different things; the text points out which are the most important.
2 Definitely – they're an important part of finding the answer to your questions.
3 No – just highlight the main trends of key differences. Any interpretation comes in the discussion section.
4 No, only the ones which show something interesting.
5 Yes.
6 Things that are similar or different. Values that are very high or low. Interesting correlations.
7 Absolutely not – make notes on the key results only.
8 Put the test name and the p value in parentheses after the result.

10a
Extract A describes visual 1; extract B describes visual 3

b
1 changed
2 are shown
3 shown as a percentage of
4 decreased
5 had the fastest consumption of H_2S
6 compared with
7 caused
8 resulted in
9 inhibition of
10 stayed high
11 increased
12 showed a linear pattern of
13 as high as
14 was seen
15 while no significant change

Unit 8

1a
1 The information in the results section highlights the key findings of the research and also any secondary findings. The discussion section explains what the results mean and how they move research in the area forward. The discussion section often also relates the current research to earlier research by the author team and/or other researchers.
2 The results section is more objective and presents the facts of what is found. The discussion is more subjective as it requires a personal interpretation of what the results mean. The two are often separated to make it clear what is fact and what is opinion.
3 The results and discussion sections may be presented together if (a) there is only one key finding in

the research; (b) the research produced a large number of results. When there is only one finding, the researcher writes the sections together because separate results and discussion sections would be very short. When there are many results, the researcher may choose to use sections with headings and subheadings to separate different parts of the research.
4 The discussion focuses on interpreting the results. A conclusion is a short summary of the whole paper.

b
A Results (the results data are presented)
B Discussion (includes interpretation of the results)
C Materials and methods (it describes process, method, equipment)

c
a Carbonisation and activation
b were performed, were contained
c The highest ...
d ranging between ... and ...
e Therefore
f will be
g examined
h attained

2a
1 ultra-thin
2 sheet
3 Fermi level
4 property of sth
5 impurity
6 layer
7 Dirac point
8 dope/dopant

b
1 carbon   2 lays the dopant onto
3 F4-TCNQ   4 negative   5 air

3a
b Effect of F4-TCNQ on monolayer graphene
(a) and (c) are both specific pieces of information: (a) is just one of Max's findings and (c) is a statement of one general truth.

b
1 The second sentence (*The doping level of the graphene layers was precisely monitored with ARPES measurements*) describes method, so it belongs in the materials and methods section. The fifth sentence (*Evidently, deposition of F4-TCNQ activated electron transfer from graphene toward the molecule thus neutralising the excess negative charge*) is an interpretation, so it belongs in the discussion section.

2 *has an effect on* in the first sentence, *is deposited* in the sixth sentence and *is observed* in the final sentence should be in the past tense (*had an effect on*, *was deposited* and *was observed*). These are reporting the results of one specific experiment (or set of experiments) conducted in the past. In sentence 3, 'the Fermi level *is located* about 0.42 eV above the Dirac point', the verb can stay in the present simple as it is talking about a general truth, rather than one particular past finding.

c
1 b
2 The other sentences give evidence for the key result.

d
Sentences a and e describe a key result.

e
(a) A comparison with the nonfluorinated version of the F4-TCNQ molecule, TCNQ, shows that the charge transfer increases significantly when the F4 is present. (c) Charge transfer occurs with TCNQ, but the Fermi energy always remains at least 0.25 eV above the Dirac point (Fig. 4a). (f) The maximum shift of the band structure is obtained for a TCNQ deposition of 0.4 nm (Fig. 4d), but no additional shift is observed for higher amounts of deposited molecules.

(e) The F4-TCNQ layer is sensitive to temperature. (b) As the temperature increased above 75 °C, the difference between the Dirac energy and the Fermi energy also increased. (d) The difference returned to the level of a graphene layer at 230 °C.

5a
1 secondary
2 visuals/data
3 research questions
4 references
5 too many words
6 headings/subheadings

c
1 As shown in Fig. 1a
2 As Fig. 1d shows
3 It can be observed in Fig. 3d that *or* In Fig. 3d, it can be observed that
4 Fig. 3d shows that

6a
Comparison: far less effective, compared to
Contrast: In contrast to, While, half that of

b
1 g   2 d   3 a   4 c   5 e
6 b   7 h   8 f

c
a noticeable, extremely, significantly, highly, considerably
b slight, minor, marginal

d
1 as can be seen in   2 contrast to
3 considerably   4 resulted in a longer   5 noticeably thicker
6 while

8b
1 Yes – comment on all the results mentioned, in the same order, and say what they mean.
2 No – if the result is important, it should be in the results section.
3 You don't need to mention the results in detail, but you probably need to refer to them. Use a noun phrase to summarise the result, then interpret the finding.
4 Yes – tie your results in to what others have done, or to other work you've done.
5 Be concise.

9a
1 movement of   2 towards
3 deposition of   4 electron transfer
5 from

b
1 The **ability of** a gecko **to** walk **on** walls demonstrates that **activation of** the adhesive system improves the gecko's movement over smooth surfaces.
2 The **formation of** a CaP layer **on** the surface allowed further crystal growth.
3 Although the species *M. fortunata* has a lower **exposure** to vent fluids it seems to have a higher **accumulation of** metals in its tissues.

c
a ... the energy difference increases, which indicates ...
b ... the energy difference increases, indicating ...
NB: A comma (,) replaces the full stop (.) before *which* or *indicating*.

d
1 The adhesive apparatus is only activated on sloped surfaces, not on flat surfaces even when slippage occurs, **which results / resulting** in greatly reduced sprinting velocity on smooth, flat surfaces.
2 Consumption of dark chocolate resulted in the decrease in the stress hormone cortisol in the urine, **which suggests / suggesting** potential benefits of dark chocolate consumption.

3 On exposure to metals, *B. azoricus* demonstrates considerable antioxidant enzymatic activity, **which reflects / reflecting** a physiological adaptation to continuous metal exposure.

11a
1 L   2 L   3 F   4 F   5 L   6 F
7 F

b
Points mentioned: 2, 3, 5, 7

12a
Limitations: The results of the present study might have been different if; Another limitation of the study is
Suggest future research: further studies are needed; it would be beneficial to investigate this further; Future research should also be encouraged to examine

b
Limitations: 1, 2, 4
Suggest future research: 3, 5

c
1 indicates   2 hoped   3 serve as
4 scope   5 permit   6 Given
7 clear   8 raises

13a
a 1   b 2, 3, 4   c 5, 6

b
As presented in several other studies, … in a previous paper, it was shown that … Recent work has suggested theoretically that …

■■■ Unit 9

1a
1 Panspermia is the hypothesis that the **seeds of life** exist all over the universe and that early life forms could have begun on other planets and travelled to Earth on **meteorites**.
3 Supporters of the hypothesis claim that a number of facts make it credible. Firstly, they believe that the fossil record shows that life forms appeared too soon after the Earth was formed for them to have begun here. Secondly, research suggests that other planets or moons contain possible habitats for life, and meteorites from Mars have been found on Earth, showing that the **vehicle** for this transport exists. Some of these meteorites have also been shown to contain molecules which are important for life. Thirdly, many **extremophile** species have been shown to survive in **harsh conditions** and so it is possible that an organism could survive in **deep space**. In fact, some bacteria, **lichens** and even a

kind of animal called a tardigrade have been able to survive in such conditions, using the surface of the planet or meteorite as a **protective layer** against **UV radiation**. Finally, some researchers claim to have discovered extraterrestrial bacteria in meteorites and living cells in air from 40 km above the Earth.

b
1 What was I investigating?
2 Why was it important?
3 What was already known about the subject of my research?
4 What did I expect to know after doing the research?
5 How did I approach the problem?

c
1 What was I investigating?
2 What was already known about the subject of my research?
3 What did I expect to know after doing the research?
4 Why was it important?
5 How did I approach the problem?

2a
4, 2, 1, 3, 5

b
1 a Could (protect); would increase
   b report
   c have investigated; have speculated
   d reported; were able to; found; decreased
2 a *would* and *could*
   b present simple
   c present perfect simple
   d past simple

3a
Q4 *Why was it important?* If sufficiently protected by meteorite-like material, microorganisms may also survive the journey through space.
Q2 *What was already known about the subject of my research?* Brandstätter *et al.* (2008) reported that microorganisms embedded in 2 cm-thick rocks on the outer surface of a re-entry capsule, simulating the entry of a meteorite, did not survive.
Q1 *What was I investigating?* The resistance of rock-colonising microbial communities and lichens to outer space conditions
Q3 *What did I expect to know after doing the research?* Further information about the resistance.
Q5 *How did I approach the problem?* In a real, in-space, experiment – during the Biopan-6 flight of ESA on board a Russian Foton satellite

b
1 have provided   2 have been
3 reported   4 did not survive   5 is

4a

Both sentences are citations (they tell us the author(s) of a research paper and what they discovered). The main difference is that in (a), the author comes first, in (b) the information comes first. Sentence (a) is *author prominent* and is written author–(date)–information. Sentence (b) is *information prominent* and is written information–(author, date).

b

1 a; c 2 b; d

c

1 demonstrate/prove
2 prove/demonstrate
3 observe   4 hypothesise
5 suggest   6 conclude   7 discover

6a

1 To get the reader's attention and encourage them to read further; to provide a concise summary of the key points of the research
2 The abstract should give the researcher enough information to know if the paper is relevant to his/her own research.
3 A sentence or two of the key points from the introduction, method, results and discussion
4 When you search for papers via a database, often all you can see initially is the abstract. In the past, a visual or heading might attract attention and encourage you to read further, but now you can't see those unless you choose to look at the whole article. The abstract therefore needs to encourage people to look at the whole paper.

b

1 D   2 A   3 C   4 B

c

D, A, C, B

The information in the abstract should be presented in the same order that the sections appear in the paper.

7a

B

b

1 F Svenja points out that you should not reference other people's work in an abstract. These references are mainly found in the introduction and discussion sections of the paper.
2 T
3 F Mya needs less methodological information in the abstract. If someone wants to know about the details of the method, they can read that section of the paper.
4 F There should not be references to figures in the abstract.
5 T

c

Current surface conditions on Mars are extremely challenging for life. The question is whether there are any features on Mars that could provide protection against the surface conditions. One possibility is that the surface material plays a protective role. With the aim of evaluating this possibility two microorganisms, *Acidithiobacillus ferrooxidans*, an acidophile, and *Deinococcus radiodurans*, a radiation-resistant microorganism, were exposed to simulated Mars conditions. Exposure was for different times under the protection of 2 and 5 mm layers of oxidised iron minerals. Survival was evaluated by growing the organisms on fresh media. Here we report that both the 2 and 5 mm thick layers provided enough protection against radiation and Mars environmental conditions for the bacteria to survive.

8a

1 The question is whether …
2 One possibility is that …
3 With the aim of evaluating this possibility …
4 Here we report that …

b

1 state the research question: a, d, f, j
2 present the hypothesis: b, i
3 introduce the method: k
4 introduce key results: c, e, g, h, l

c

1 Those   2 that   3 that   4 those
5 that

10b

Good advice: e, f, g
Bad advice: a, b ,c, d

d

1 Title 4: Protection for *Acidithiobacillus ferrooxidans* and *Deinococcus radiodurans* exposed to simulated Mars environmental conditions by surface material
2 It's too long.
3 It includes the key finding.

e

Title 1: Jokes are unclear (vague); the readers may not understand the joke; the joke probably won't include important keywords for an internet search
Title 2: It is not clear (vague); a question in the title does not say what the key results were
Title 3: The title is too general (imprecise); it does not say what kind of organism; it does not say what kind of protection; the title says what the researcher did, but not what the key result was.

Advice: Include keywords for internet searches; say what the key result of the research was; include details about what was studied or where the research happened; avoid using phrases like 'A study of …'.

11a

a The data suggest that
b 'from' is used in *are protected from* to describe the thing that causes the damage; 'for' is used in *protection for* to describe that thing which receives the protection from any possible damage.
c *exposed*. Title 4 is a noun phrase and 'exposed' is a short form for *which are exposed*.

b

1 Modification
2 variation
3 Activation
4 detection

13b

A 2   B 4   C 3   D 1   E 7   F 6
G 8   H 5

14a

The style of the underlined words and phrases in the letter is not appropriate.

b

1 enclosed
2 manuscript entitled
3 submitting for the exclusive consideration of
4 extends the research
5 therefore be of interest to those in the field of
6 Knowledgeable referees for this paper might include
7 I would prefer that … not be approached to referee this research.
8 your consideration of my work
9 address all correspondence concerning this manuscript

Unit 10

1b

1 Anyone who works in malaria research; pharmaceutical companies
2 No – if a researcher wants to submit an abstract, he/she must apply before 4 April.
3 Go to the website www.eimr.org/con7

c

1 application **deadline**
2 on a **strictly** first-come, first-served **basis**
3 **keynote** speakers
4 online **registration** only
5 poster **presentation**
6 **preliminary** programme
7 **registration** fees
8 to **submit** an abstract
9 in due **course**
10 check back for **updates**

d

a 5   b 6   c 10   d 7   e 9   f 4
g 1   h 3   i 2   j 8

2b

a 1   b 4   c 5   d 6   e 3   f 2

c

Suggested answer
In his talk, Milan mentions that counting IFN-γ secreting T cells using the *ex vivo* IFN-γ ELISPOT is the method that has been used. His research investigates an alternative, the use of flow cytometry and RT-PCR to detect the secretion of MIG (CXCL9), a cytokine secreted by T cells.

3a

1 Good afternoon, everybody.
2 I'd like to start by thanking you
3 My name is Milan Poborski and
4 I'm going to talk today
5 To start with, I'll explain
6 After that, I'll
7 Finally, I will discuss
8 I plan to talk for about 40 minutes, leaving plenty of time for

b

a 8   b 1   c 4   d 3   e 5, 6, 7
f 2

c

His presentation is organised in the same order as a research paper: he is going to give an <u>introduction</u> to the problems with other methods, describe the <u>method</u> he used and the <u>results</u> he got, and finally he will <u>discuss</u> his key results.

4a

1 c   2 a   3 b   4 d   5 e

b

a Let's begin by looking at
b That's all I have to say about … so now I'd like to move on to
c As I have already said
d I will be returning to those shortly.
e As you can see from this image

c

1 c   2 d   3 b   4 e   5 a

d

1 As I mentioned earlier
2 I'll deal with this point later.
3 We've looked at … so now let's turn to
4 the charts here indicate
5 Next we'll look at

6a

d, c, a, e, b

b

1 **So let me** recap what I've said.
2 I therefore **believe** that …
3 That **brings me** to the end of my talk today.
4 I would like to thank you for **being such an** attentive audience
5 I would be happy to **answer any questions** you may have.

8c

Conversation 1: b, c
Conversation 2: g, h
Conversation 3: d, h
Conversation 4: e, g, h
Conversation 5: a
Conversation 6: f
Conversation 7: b
Conversation 8: d, h

9a

1 How
2 honest
3 this
4 based
5 looking
6 giving
7 about
8 go
9 turnout
10 sessions
11 face
12 forward

10a

1 1, 4, 6, 8
2 2, 3, 5, 7

b

4 and 5 are unsuitable in English-speaking cultures because they are too direct. 8 might be unsuitable in some situations, especially if the phrase is used without an introduction or greeting such as 'Hello' or 'Hi'.

12b

1 title
2 simple
3 abstract
4 contact
5 columns
6 text
7 heading
8 Number
9 white space
10 sentences
11 font
12 colours

c

1 Both posters are well organised.
2 There is space around the sections in both posters.
3 Title and section headings are clear.

14a

1 F – Mosi refers to 'most studies so far' which suggests more than a few have been done.
2 T
3 F – Mosi used human volunteers who had not had malaria.
4 T
5 T

b

1 It seems then that
2 My research though focuses on
3 most studies so far have
4 As you can see in this chart, / The second graph shows
5 In this study,

15a

• Could you just clarify …   Answer C
• Can you tell me …   Answer B
• I can't remember …   Answer A

b

1 **Is that what you wanted to know about** them?
2 **If you want to know more about** the specifics of the protocol or the reagents I used, **just send me an email**. The address is here, on this handout and on my card.
3 **Does that answer your** question?

GLOSSARY

This glossary contains useful words and phrases from the texts and audioscripts. The numbers in brackets refer to the unit(s) in which they appear. Key: v = verb; n = noun; adj = adjective; adv = adverb; cc = collocation [a collocation is a common combination of words]; sby = somebody; sth = something

Word	Definition	Translation
achieve (1, 6)	v to succeed in finishing something (especially something difficult)	
activate (4, 8, 9)	v to cause something to start	
adapt (to sth) (1, 4, 5, 7, 9)	v to change something according to a different environment or for a different purpose	
adaptation (1, 7, 8)	n the process (or the result of a process) of changing according to a different environment or for a different purpose	
adhesive (3)	n glue adj something that can be glued	
adjust (4, 5)	v to change something slightly	
adsorb (4, 9)	v to hold molecules of a gas or liquid on the surface	
alloy (4)	n a metal that is made by mixing two or more metals or a metal and another substance	
alter (8, 9)	v to change something, usually slightly	
alternative (3, 4, 8, 9, 10)	n a different plan or method which can be used instead of another one adj something that is different from something else	
ambient temperature (5)	cc room temperature or the normal temperature of a particular object or environment	
amperage (6)	n the strength of an electrical current measured in amperes	
antigen (10)	n a substance that causes an immune response in the body, often by the production of antibodies	
anxiety (2, 8)	n an uncomfortable feeling of nervousness or worry	
apparatus (4, 5, 8)	n equipment or tools for a particular purpose	
approach (1, 2, 4, 8, 9)	v 1 to deal with something 2 to speak to, write to, or visit somebody in order to do something n a method of doing or thinking about something	
aquarium (7)	n a man-made environment where fish, other water animals and plants can be kept and studied	
arrange a meeting (3)	cc to organise a meeting	
assess (1, 2, 4, 5, 7, 9)	v to judge or decide the amount, value, quality or importance of something	
assessment (2)	n a judgment or decision about the amount, value, quality or importance of something	
attenuated (10)	adj weakened	
automatically (5)	adv independently (without human control)	
availability (1)	n the fact that somebody is free to work, be contacted, go to meetings, etc.	
(be) affected (by sth) (5, 7)	cc to be changed or influenced by somebody or something	
(be) attentive (to sth) (10)	cc 1 interested 2 listening carefully	
(be) composed (of sth) (4, 9)	cc to be formed or made from something	
(be) involved (in sth) (1, 2, 5, 8)	cc 1 to be included 2 to be made a part of something	
(be) made up of (sth) (3)	cc to be composed of or formed from something	
(be) of interest (to sby) (7)	cc interesting	

Word	Definition	Translation
(be) on track (4)	cc making progress and likely to succeed	
(be) relevant (to sth) (1, 2, 3, 4, 6, 8)	cc connected with what is happening or being discussed	
(be) representative (of sth) (7)	cc sharing characteristics or features which are typical of a group of people, situations or things	
(be) resistant (to sth) (5, 7, 9)	adj not affected, influenced or damaged by something	
(be) selective (for sth) (8)	cc choosing some things but not others, often for a reason	
(be) sensitive (to sth) (1, 8, 10)	adj affected, influenced or damaged by something	
(be) unresponsive (to sth) (5)	adj not responsive to something (= does not react to something)	
benchwork (1)	n work done in the laboratory rather than in the natural environment	
benefit (4)	n a good or positive effect	
bind (to sth) (6, 7, 10)	v to stick to, combine with, or form a bond with something	
blind trial (2)	cc a type of clinical trial where the patient and researcher do not know which patients are receiving the medicine and which a placebo	
break down (into sth) (3)	v to reduce into smaller parts	
calibrate (5)	v to set a machine to a standard scale	
capsule (6, 9)	n a small container	
carry out (2, 5, 6, 8)	v to do or complete something, especially something you have planned to do	
characteristic (5, 7)	n a typical or noticeable quality of somebody or something	
classify (sth as sth) (2, 9)	v to divide things into groups according to their type	
clinical trial (2)	cc a controlled test of a new drug on human subjects	
clone (1)	v to create a genetic copy of a plant or animal n a genetic copy of a plant or animal that has the same gene as the original plant or animal	
coat (sth with sth) (3, 5, 6)	v to cover something with a thin layer of something	
collaborate (with sby on sth) (3)	v to work with somebody for a specific purpose	
come up with (4)	v to suggest or think of an idea or plan	
comment (on sth) (1, 8, 9)	v to say or write something which expresses an opinion	
commercial application (commercial use) (1, 2, 6, 7, 8)	cc a way to use a device, finding etc. which could make money for a company	
commonly (6, 7)	adv usually	
complicated (3)	adj 1 formed of many different parts 2 difficult to understand	
composition analysis (5)	cc a procedure to discover what something is made of	
compound (3, 5, 6, 7)	n a substance formed from a combination of two or more elements	
concentrate a solution (4)	cc to make a liquid or substance stronger by removing water from it or by adding more solute	
concentrate (on sth) (1, 4)	v to focus your attention on something	
concentration (1, 4, 5, 6, 7, 8)	n the strength of a solution, especially the amount of solute in a fixed volume of solvent	
condense (3, 4, 6)	v to change state from a gas to a liquid	

Word	Definition	Translation
conduct (4, 5, 6)	**v** to transmit heat or electricity through a substance	
considerable (6, 8)	**adj** of large or noticeable importance	
consistent (6, 7, 8)	**adj** always the same or always behaving in the same or a similar way	
constant (4)	**adj** staying the same and not changing	
consumption (2, 7, 8, 9)	**n** the amount of something used	
contain (3, 4, 5, 6, 8, 9)	**v** 1 to have something inside something else 2 to include something	
contaminated (7, 9)	**adj** not clean or not pure (pure = not mixed with anything)	
control group (2)	**cc** a group in an experiment which do not receive the treatment, procedure etc.	
controversial (9)	**adj** causing disagreement or discussion	
convection (4)	**n** the transfer of heat in a gas or liquid by the heated part moving upwards	
critique (2)	**n** a report which examines somebody's work or ideas very carefully	
cross (sth) out (5)	**v** to draw a line through a text or picture, usually because it is wrong	
cytokine (10)	**n** a protein released by a cell which has an effect on other cells or on the communication between cells	
deal with (7, 9, 10)	**v** to take action in order to solve a problem	
depict (7)	**v** to represent or show something in a diagram, picture or story	
detect (1, 3, 4, 9, 10)	**v** to discover something using special tools and/or a special method	
device (2, 3, 6)	**n** an object or machine that has been designed for a specific purpose	
diffract (4)	**v** to cause light to divide into the various colours of the spectrum	
diffraction (5)	**n** the spreading of light into its various colours as it passes through a small opening	
dilute (4, 6)	**v** to make a liquid or other substance less concentrated (weaker) by mixing it with something else	
dimension (1, 4)	**n** a measurement of something in a particular direction, especially its height, length or width	
dip (sth in sth) (6, 8)	**v** to put something into a liquid for a short time	
dissolve (4, 5, 6, 7)	**v** 1 (of a solid) to be absorbed by a liquid 2 (of a liquid) to absorb a solid	
distribution (1, 9)	**n** the amounts or the way in which things are divided or spread out in a place	
do a run (5)	**cc** to complete an experiment	
dosage (6)	**n** an amount of something needed for a specific purpose	
dummy (2)	**adj** not real	
durability (1)	**n** hardness or the ability to remain undamaged for a long time	
effective (1, 2, 3, 7, 8, 9)	**adj** successful at achieving a specific result	
embed (2, 5, 6, 9)	**v** to fix something into a substance	
enhance (3, 9)	**v** to improve the quality, amount or strength of something	
enthalpy (6)	**n** the total amount of heat or chemical energy in a system	
enzyme (1, 7)	**n** a chemical substance which causes a chemical reaction to happen or to happen faster without changing itself	
equation (7)	**n** a mathematical statement	
essential (7)	**adj** necessary	
evaporation (8)	**n** the process or the result of a process of a liquid becoming a gas	
evidence (2, 3, 8, 9)	**n** one or more reasons to believe that something is or is not true	
exclude (3)	**v** 1 to stop something becoming a part of something else 2 to not include something	

Word	Definition	Translation
expand (5)	v to increase	
experimental set-up (4,5)	cc the equipment and procedures used in an experiment	
exposure (to sth) (4, 7, 8, 9)	n experiencing something (often something harmful or unpleasant) by being in a particular place or situation	
extreme (7, 8, 9)	adj very large in amount or degree	
field (1)	n an area of activity, interest or study	
fieldwork (1)	n research done in the natural environment not in the laboratory	
filter (sth) out (6)	v to remove something from something else	
flex (6)	n a cable which carries an electric current to a piece of electronic equipment	
focus (on sth) (1, 3, 6, 8, 9, 10)	v to give a lot of attention to somebody or something n the main point of interest	
follow-up (3, 5)	n a further action connected with something that happened before	
functionalise (6)	v to make functional or to adapt or prepare something for a specific purpose	
fuse together (6)	v to join or become combined	
gather (1)	v to collect different things, often from different places or people	
generate (1, 2, 5, 8)	v 1 to cause something to exist 2 to produce energy in a particular form	
genetically engineered organism (4)	cc a living thing whose genetic structured has been changed for a particular reason or purpose	
gills (7)	n the organ which fish and other water creatures use to take in oxygen	
give (sth) a go (1)	cc to try to do something which may or may not be successful	
give (sth) up (1)	v to stop doing something	
graduate (1)	n a person who has completed a course of study such as a degree from a university or college	
grind (into a powder) (6)	v to break a solid into extremely small pieces	
habitat (1, 4)	n the natural environment of a living creature	
hang on (5, 7)	v to wait for a short time	
harvest (sth from sth) (3)	v to collect something	
have an effect (on sth) (2, 4, 5, 8, 9)	cc to influence something	
hormone (2, 4, 8, 9)	n a chemical substance produced in the body that controls the activity of certain cells or organs	
host (2)	n an animal or plant on or in which another organism lives	
hydraulic (5)	adj operated by or involving the pressure of a liquid	
hydrostatic (5)	adj relating to fluids which are not moving or to the pressures they produce	
hydrothermal vent (7)	cc a gap in the floor of the ocean which produces a flow of warm water	
hypothesis (2, 4, 9)	n an idea or explanation for something which is based on known facts but has not yet been proved	
identical (2)	adj exactly the same or very similar	
impedance (6)	n a measure of the power of a piece of electrical equipment to stop the flow of a current	
impede (1)	v to slow down a process or make something more difficult to do	
implication (9)	n the effect that an action will have on something else in the future	
impurity (8)	n a low quality substance that is mixed with something else and makes it less pure	
in the context of (10)	cc when a particular situation or condition exists	
in vitro (2)	adv happening in artificial conditions such as a test tube	
in vivo (3, 10)	adv happening in a living organism	

Word	Definition	Translation
incidence (of sth) (4)	**n** 1 the frequency at which something happens 2 an event	
inconsistent (5, 8)	**adj** if something is *inconsistent*, different parts of it do not agree, or it does not agree with something else	
incubation (6)	**n** a process which allows something to be kept at a constant temperature for a particular amount of time	
indication (7)	**n** a sign that something is true, exists, or is likely to happen	
indicator (of sth) (1, 10)	**n** something that shows what a situation is like	
inevitable (8)	**adj** certain to happen, something that cannot be prevented	
influence (3, 4)	**v** to have an effect on something or someone	
informative (9)	**adj** providing a lot of useful information	
inhibit (2, 9)	**v** to prevent something from happening or to slow down a process	
inspire (3)	**v** to give somebody the idea for something	
institution (1, 2)	**n** a large and important organisation, such as a university or a bank	
internalise (6)	**v** to bring inside	
interpret (2)	**v** to decide on the most likely meaning of something	
interpretation (7, 8)	**n** an understanding or explanation of a situation or thing	
interrupt (3, 4, 10)	**v** 1 to stop a person from speaking for a short period by something you say or do 2 to stop something from happening for a limited amount of time	
isolate (5, 6, 9)	**v** to separate something from other things, often things that are normally combined	
jargon (9)	**n** special words or phrases used by particular groups of people, especially in their work	
join in (3, 10)	**v** to become involved in an activity (such as a conversation)	
keep (sth) in mind (8)	**cc** to remember a fact or piece of information when you are making a decision	
lengthen (8)	**v** to make longer	
linear (5, 7)	**adj** 1 relating to a relationship between two things that is clear and direct 2 consisting of or related to lines	
link (4, 5)	**n** a connection between two people, ideas or things	
load (sth into sth) (5)	**v** to put something into something (usually a machine)	
long-term (1, 2)	**adj** continuing for a long time into the future	
look through (6)	**v** to read something quickly	
magnitude (3)	**n** the large size or importance of something	
mesh (6, 8)	**n** a piece of material like a net with small spaces in it, made from wire, plastic or thread	
metabolic (2, 8, 9)	**adj** connected to chemical processes of the body	
microbiota (2)	**n** the microorganisms that live in a particular part of the body	
mimic (3)	**v** to copy the way in which someone or something behaves	
mixture (of sth) (5)	**n** a substance made from a combination of substances	
mortality (7)	**n** the number of deaths in a group in a particular period of time	
motion (3, 4)	**n** 1 the act or process of moving 2 an action or a movement	
multi-disciplinary (3)	**adj** of an activity which involves different subjects of study (such as physics and chemistry)	
narrow (sth) down (9)	**v** to make a number or list of things smaller and clearer by removing things that are least important or least likely to happen	
navigate (1)	**v** to find a way over an area of land or water	
negotiate terrain (1)	**v** to manage to travel over a difficult physical environment	
network (2)	**v** to meet people who might be useful to know, especially for your work or studies	

Word	Definition	Translation
nozzle (5)	**n** a narrow opening at the end of a tube which allows gas or liquid to be delivered to a particular place	
numerous (5)	**adj** many	
objective (6)	**adj** based on facts and not influenced by personal feelings or beliefs	
obstacle (1)	**n** 1 something that prevents movement 2 a process which makes something more difficult to do	
odour (1, 8)	**n** a smell	
one-on-one (3)	**adj** a meeting between two people, usually between a teacher and a student	
online forum (2)	**n** a place on the Internet where people can leave messages or discuss particular subjects with other people	
optimal conditions (4)	**cc** the perfect environment for something to happen	
organism (4, 6, 7, 9)	**n** a single living plant, animal, virus etc.	
orient (3)	**v** to move something so that it rests in a particular location or points in a particular direction	
outcome (1, 5)	**n** a result	
outline (1, 10)	**v** to give the main facts about something	
output (6, 9)	**n** an amount of something produced by a process	
overview (of sth) (6)	**n** a short description of something which provides general information without details	
participant (2, 4, 10)	**n** a person who takes part in an activity	
peer review (2)	**cc** a critical review of research by experienced professionals	
permanent (1)	**adj** lasting for a long time or forever	
phase (1, 4, 8, 10)	**n** any stage in a series of events or in a process of development	
physiology (1, 2)	**n** (the scientific study of) the way in which the bodies of living things work	
place (3, 5, 6)	**v** to put something in a particular position	
placebo (2)	**n** a substance given to someone who is told that it is a particular medicine, either to make them feel as if they are getting better or to compare the effect of the particular medicine when given to others	
porous (4)	**adj** describes something that has many small holes, so liquid or gas can pass through it	
precipitation (5)	**n** when a solid substance is produced from a liquid during a chemical process	
preferred method (10)	**cc** the method usually used	
presence (of sth) (3, 9)	**n** when something is found in a particular place	
proportion (7)	**n** the number or amount of a group or part of something when compared to the whole	
propose (sth to sby) (4)	**v** to suggest a possible plan or action for other people to consider	
prospective observational study (2)	**cc** a study in which one group of people who receive a particular treatment are followed over time and compared with another group of people who did not receive the treatment	
protein (2, 5, 6, 7, 9)	**n** an organic combination of amino acids	
protocol (2, 4, 5, 10)	**n** 1 a set of rules for doing something 2 the method to be followed when doing a scientific experiment	
provide an insight (into sth) (2)	**cc** to give a clear understanding of something	
publication (1, 9)	**n** the process of presenting research to the scientific community, usually in a journal	
pulse (6)	**n** an amount of sound, light, or electricity that continues for a short time and is usually repeated	
pulsed (3)	**adj** happening for repeated, short periods of time, rather than working continuously	
pump (sth) up (5)	**v** to fill something with a gas or liquid	

Word	Definition	Translation
purify (6)	v to remove dirty or harmful substances from something	
purity (5)	n the quality or state of being pure or clean	
put (sby) off (doing) (sth) (1)	cc 1 to make someone dislike something or someone 2 to persuade someone not to do something	
randomised (1)	adj by chance and not according to a plan	
range (between n^1 and n^2) (from n^1 to n^2) (6, 8)	v to have an upper and a lower limit	
range (of sth) (2, 6, 8, 9, 10)	n 1 the amount, number or type of something between an upper and a lower limit 2 a set of similar things	
rapid (5, 8)	adj fast or sudden	
ratio (of sth to sth) (4, 5, 6, 8)	n the relationship between two groups or amounts, which shows how much bigger one is than the other	
raw data (2, 7)	cc experimental results which have not yet been analysed	
reach a plateau (5)	cc to come to a point at which change or development stops	
read up on a topic (3)	cc to research a subject in detail	
reagent (5, 10)	n a substance used in a chemical reaction to detect, measure, examine, or produce other substances	
recap (10)	v to repeat the main points of an explanation or description	
receptor (6, 8, 10)	n a molecule in a cell or on the surface of a cell which something (e.g. a hormone, a drug) can bind to	
relate (to sth) (2, 3, 4, 5, 8)	v to find or show a connection between two or more things	
rely on (1, 4)	v to need a particular thing in order to do something	
replicate (1, 4)	v to make or do something again in exactly the same way	
reproduce the data (4)	cc to get the same results as before by repeating an experiment	
requirement (5)	n something that must be done	
reset (5)	v to prepare a machine so that it can be operated in a particular way or to return it to its original settings	
resistance (to sth) (6, 8, 9)	n showing little or no reaction to a process or to a particular situation	
response (to sth) (3, 4, 5, 9, 10)	n 1 a reaction to a process 2 a formal answer to a question or suggestion	
rinse (with sth) (6)	v to remove a substance from something or clean something using a liquid	
rule (sth) out (1,5)	v to decide that something is impossible or will not happen	
run (sby) through (sth) (6)	cc to tell someone about something so that they can give their advice or opinion on it	
run (sth) through (sth) (4, 6)	v to pass a gas or liquid through something	
saturate (5)	v to add one substance to another until no more can be added	
scale (7)	n the size or level of something	
scale (sth) up (3)	v to increase the size, amount or importance of something, usually a process	
schedule (1)	v to arrange a meeting or other activity for a particular time or day	
schematic view (5)	cc an image showing the main parts of something in a simple way	
secrete (10)	v to produce and release a liquid	
sense (1)	v to experience or detect physical things n an ability to understand, recognise or react to something, especially something that can be seen, heard, tasted, smelled or felt	
sensitive information (2)	cc secret information	
sequence word (5)	cc words which show the order in which something happens (e.g. then, after that)	

Word	Definition	Translation
shear force (3)	cc stress applied parallel to a surface of a material	
significant (7, 8)	adj 1 important or noticeable 2 probably caused by something other than chance	
simulate (1, 3, 4, 9)	v to do or make something in a similar or the same way as something else	
simultaneous (9)	adj happening at the same time	
sketch (sth out) (4, 7, 9)	v to make a drawing or give a short description of something using only a few details	
slide (3)	v to move or cause to move easily over a surface	
slide (6, 7)	n a small piece of glass on which you can put something in order to look at it through a microscope	
soil (1)	n the material on the surface of the earth in which plants grow	
solubility (5)	n the ability to be dissolved to form a solution	
specialism (2)	n an area within a subject of study such as molecular biology in biology	
species (2, 7, 8, 9)	n a set of animals or plants in which members share similar characteristics	
specimen (5)	n 1 something shown or examined as an example 2 a typical example of something	
speculate (about/on sth) (9)	v to guess the possible answer to a question or cause of a situation	
speed (1, 6, 8)	n how fast something happens or moves	
stable (1, 8)	adj not likely to move or change or react	
stage (1, 4, 5, 6)	n a part of an activity or process	
stain (2, 5, 6)	v to add a reagent or a dye (dye = a substance used to change the colour of something) to a specimen in order to make it easier to see a particular thing through a microscope	
stand alone (7)	v to be presented separately	
stand out (10)	v to be very noticeable	
stick (to sth) (2,3,4)	v to cause something to become fixed	
stick with (4)	v to continue to do something in a way that you have used before	
submit (sth) to (sby) (1, 2, 9, 10)	cc to give or offer something for a decision to be made by others	
subsequent (5)	adj happening after something else	
sufficient (9)	adj enough for a particular purpose	
supervise (1)	v to watch a person or activity to make certain that everything is done correctly	
surface area (8)	cc the total amount of space the outside surface(s) of an object covers	
suspension (6)	n a liquid mixture which contains very small pieces of solid material	
take (sth) up (7)	v to absorb something or to use something	
talk (sby) through (sth) (2, 4, 6)	cc to explain a procedure to someone in the correct order	
target (6, 9)	v to direct something to a particular location n a place you want to reach	
technique (2, 3, 9)	n a way of doing an activity	
texture (3)	n the quality of a surface: the degree to which a surface is hard, soft, smooth, rough etc.	
that makes sense (4, 7)	cc that is a good idea	
theoretically (8)	adv in a way that agrees with some rule or hypothesis	
threshold (6)	n the level at which something starts to happen or have an effect	
to some degree (5)	cc to a certain amount, partly	

Word	Definition	Translation
tolerance (7)	n the amount of pain, heat, difficulty etc. which something can suffer without being harmed	
track (3)	v to follow the movement of something	
transfer (from sth to sth) (1, 3)	v to move (someone or something) from one place to another	
transition zone (5)	cc the part of the Earth's structure located below the crust and upper mantle but above the lower mantle	
treatment (1, 3, 4, 9)	n a particular chemical, procedure or situation etc. which is given to one group in an experiment to see how that group is affected	
trend (7)	n a general pattern of development or change in a situation or in the way something behaves	
trial (2)	n a test, usually over a limited period of time, to discover how effective or suitable something is	
trigger (3)	v to make something start suddenly	
tumour (2, 6)	n a mass of cells which are not normal	
ultraviolet radiation (9)	cc energy with wavelengths shorter than light we can see, but longer than X-rays	
undergo (3)	v to experience a powerful force or something unpleasant	
uninhabitable (9)	adj not suitable or possible to live in	
uptake (4, 6, 7)	n the rate or act of taking something in	
urine (2, 8)	n a waste liquid from the body	
use (sth) alongside (sth) (10)	cc to use with or at the same time as something else	
vaccination (10)	n the process of giving someone a substance which prevents them from getting a disease	
vague (9)	adj not clear in shape or meaning	
vapour (3, 6)	n gas or extremely small drops of liquid	
verify (2, 5)	v to prove or to make certain that something exists or is true	
vibratory (3)	adj making small movements very quickly	
vice versa (7)	adv used to show that what you have just said is also true in the opposite situation	
visible spectrum (4)	cc the part of the whole energy range that we can see	
volunteer (9, 10)	n a person who agrees to do something	
work (sth) out (1, 3, 4, 5, 7, 8)	v to do a calculation to get an answer to a question or to do or develop something in a particular way	
write (sth) up (6)	v to write something in a complete or final form using notes you have made	
yield (5)	v to change shape because of the force on an object	
yield strength (5, 9)	cc the amount of stress which can be put on an object before it changes shape	
your first impression (of sth) (10)	cc your first feeling, opinion or idea about something or someone	
your intended audience (9)	cc the people who some particular information has been prepared for	
zone (5)	n an area or region which has a particular feature or characteristic that makes it different from other parts	

Acknowledgements

The authors and publishers acknowledge the following sources of copyright material and are grateful for the permissions granted. While every effort has been made, it has not always been possible to identify the sources of all the material used, or to trace all copyright holders. If any omissions are brought to our notice, we will be happy to include the appropriate acknowledgements on reprinting.

Medical Research Council Molecular Biology Laboratory, Cambridge for the adapted text on p20, 'Technology Transfer Alert!' by Tony Hodge; Macmillan Publishers Ltd for the material on pp26, 93, 'Water capture by a desert beetle', Copyright 2001; David S. Draper for adapted text on pp 39–40, 96 'Multi-anvil Press', Copyright 2011; Hilder, T.A. and Hill, J.M. for the adapted material on pp46–48, 97–98, 110, Encapsulation of the anticancer drug cisplatin into nanotubes', In Proceedings of ICONN2008, pp109–112, 2008; Hilder, T.A. and Hill, J.M. Modelling the loading and unloading of drugs into nanotubes. Small 2009, Vol. 5, pp. 300–308; John Wiley & Sons Ltd for the adapted text on pp55–56, 99, 'Adaptation to metal toxicity: a comparison of hydrothermal vent and coastal shrimps' by Gonzalez-Rey, Serafim, Company & Bebianno; Elsevier for the adapted text on pp 72, 114, 'Survival of lichens and bacteria exposed to outer space conditions – Results of the Lithopanspermia experiments' taken from 'Icarus', August 2010 by Rosa de la Torre, Leopoldo G. Sancho, Gerda Horneck, Asunción de los Ríos, Jacek Wierzchos, Karen Olsson-Francis, Charles S. Cockell, Petra Rettberg, Thomas Berger, Jean-Pierre P. de Vera, Sieglinde Ott, Jesus Martinez Frías, et al; Elsevier for the material on pp 58–59, 61, 'Metabolic rates and thermal tolerances of chemoautotrophic symbioses from Lau Basin hydrothermal vents and their implications for species distributions' taken from 'Deep Sea Research Part I: Oceanographic Research Papers' Volume 55, Issue 5, May 2008, Pages 679–695, by Michael S. Henry, James J. Childress, Dijanna Figueroa; Elsevier for the material on pp 58–60, 112, 'Metal concentrations in the shell of Bathymodiolus azoricus from contrasting hydrothermal vent fields on the mid-Atlantic ridge' taken from 'Marine Environmental Research' May 2008, by A. Cravo, P. Foster, C. Almeida, M.J. Bebianno, R. Company; Elsevier for the material on pp58, 60, 112, 'Biology of the Lucky Strike hydrothermal field' taken from 'Deep Sea Research Part I: Oceanographic Research Papers' September 1996, by Cindy Lee Van Dover, Daniel Desbruyères, Michel Segonzac, Thierry Comtet, Luiz Saldanha, Aline Fiala-Medioni, Charles Langmuir; Elsevier for the material on p58, 'Metal concentrations and metallothionein-like protein levels in deepsea fishes captured near hydrothermal vents in the Mid-Atlantic Ridge off Azores' taken from 'Deep Sea Research Part I: Oceanographic Research Papers' July 2010, by R. Company, H. Felícia, A. Serafim, A.J. Almeida, M. Biscoito, M.J. Bebianno; Elsevier for the material on p58, 'Spermatogenesis of Bathymodiolus azoricus in captivity matching reproductive behaviour at deep-sea hydrothermal vents' taken from 'Journal of Experimental Marine Biology and Ecology' 25 July 2006, by Enikö Kádár, Alexandre Lobo-da-Cunha, Ricardo S. Santos, Paul Dando; Elsevier for the material on p58, 'Variations in deep-sea hydrothermal vent communities on the Mid-Atlantic Ridge near the Azores plateau' taken from 'Deep Sea Research Part I: Oceanographic Research Papers' May 2001, by D. Desbruyères, M. Biscoito, J. -C. Caprais, A. Colaço, T. Comtet, P. Crassous, Y. Fouquet, A. Khripounoff, N. Le Bris, K. Olu, R. Riso, P. -M. Sarradin, M. Segonzac, A. Vangriesheim; Elsevier for the material on p58, 'Deep-sea and shallow-water hydrothermal vent communities: Two different phenomena?' taken from 'Chemical Geology' 15 December 2005 by V.G. Tarasov, A.V. Gebruk, A.N. Mironov, L.I. Moskalev; Elsevier for the material on pp58, 66, 'Distribution of micro-essential (Fe, Cu, Zn) and toxic (Hg) metals in tissues of two nutritionally distinct hydrothermal shrimps' taken from 'Science of The Total Environment' 1 April 2006 by Enikö Kádár, Valentina Costa, Ricardo S. Santos; Elsevier for the material on pp60–61, 'Effect of cadmium, copper and mercury on antioxidant enzyme activities and lipid peroxidation in the gills of the hydrothermal vent mussel *Bathymodiolus azoricus'* taken from 'Marine Environmental Research' August-December 2004, by R. Company, A. Serafim, M. J. Bebianno, R. Cosson, B. Shillito, A. Fiala-Médioni; C. Coletti, C. Riedl, D. S. Lee, B. Krauss, L. Patthey, K. von Klitzing, J. H. Smet, and U. Starke for the adapted material on pp64, 65, 69, 113, 'Charge neutrality and band-gap tuning of epitaxial graphene on SiC by molecular doping'; Ulrike Bauer and Walter Federle, for the material on p89 'Insect Aquaplaning: Wetness-based activiation of traps in Nepenthes pitcher plants', Insect Biomechanics Group, Department of Zoology, University of Cambridge; Greg Savage, Blake Johnson, Genevieve McArthur, Megan Willis and Stuart Lee for the material on p90 'ERP measures of material specificity for crossmodal relational memory', Macquarie Centre for Cognitive Science, Macquarie University.

Bibliography

A. Abdelouas, Y. Lu, W. Lutze and H. E. Nuttall, 'Reduction of U(VI) to U(IV) by indigenous bacteria in contaminated ground water', *Journal of Contaminant Hydrology*, 35 (1–3) (1998), 217–33

A. Cravo, P. Foster, C. Almeida, M. J. Bebianno and R. Company, 'Metal concentrations in the shell of *Bathymodiolus azoricus* from contrasting hydrothermal vent fields on the mid-Atlantic ridge', *Marine Environmental Research*, 65 (4) (2008), 338–48

A. E. Zurita, L. H. Soibelzon, E. Soibelzon, G. M. Gasparini, M. M. Cenizo and H. Arzani, 'Accessory protection structures in Glyptodon Owen (*Xenarthra, Cingulata, Glyptodontidae*)', *Annales de Paléontologie*, 96 (1) (2010), 1–11

A. El Albani, S. Bengtson, D. E. Canfield, A. Bekker, R. Macchiarelli, A. Mazurier, E. U. Hammarlund, P. Boulvais, J-J. Dupuy, C. Fontaine, F. T. Fürsich, F. Gauthier-Lafaye, P. Janvier, E. Javaux, F. Ossa Ossa, A-C Pierson-Wickmann, A. Riboulleau, P. Sardini, D. Vachard, M. Whitehouse and A. Meunier, 'Large colonial organisms with coordinated growth in oxygenated environments 2.1 Gyr ago', *Nature*, 466 (2010), 100–4

A. Kurella and N. B. Dahotre, 'Laser induced hierarchical calcium phosphate structures', *Acta Biomaterialia*, 2 (6) (2006), 677–83

A. Malladi and P. M. Hirst, 'Increase in fruit size of a spontaneous mutant of 'Gala' apple (*Malusxdomestica Borkh.*) is facilitated by altered cell production and enhanced cell size', *Journal of Experimental Botany*, 61 (11) (2010), 3003–13

A. R. Parker and C. R. Lawrence, 'Water capture by a desert beetle', *Nature*, 414 (2001), 33–4

A. Sousa, P. García-Murillo, J. Morales and L. García-Barrón, 'Anthropogenic and natural effects on the coastal lagoons in the southwest of Spain (Doñana National Park)', *ICES Journal of Marine Science* 66 (7) (2009) 1508–14

A.J. Phillips, P.A. Robinson, D.J Kedziora and R.G.Abeysuriya, 'Mammalian sleep dynamics: how diverse features arise from a common physiological framework', *Public Library of Science: Computational Biology* 6(6):e1000826 (2010), http://www.ncbi.nlm.nih.gov/pubmed/20585613

A.P. Russell and T.E. Higham, 'A new angle on clinging in geckos: incline, not substrate, triggers the deployment of the adhesive system', *Proceedings of the Royal Society B*, 276 (2009), 3705–9

B. M. Kim, S. Qian and H. H. Bau, 'Filling Carbon Nanotubes with Particles', *Nano Letters*, 5 (5) (2005), 873–78

B. Sinha and M. Fraunholz, '*Staphylococcus aureus* host cell invasion and post-invasion events', *International Journal of Medical Microbiology*, 300 (2–3) (2010), 170–75

B. W. Alto and S. A. Juliano, 'Precipitation and Temperature Effects on Populations of *Aedes albopictus (Diptera: Culicidae)*: Implications for Range Expansion', *Journal of Medical Entomology*, 38 (5) (2001), 646–56

B. Zhao, N. Pesika, H. Zeng, Z. Wei, Y. Chen, K. Autumn, K. Turner and J. Israelachvili, 'Role of Tilted Adhesion Fibrils (Setae) in the Adhesion and Locomotion of Gecko-like Systems', *Journal of Phyical Chemistry B*, 113 (12) (2009), 3615–21

C. Coletti, C. Riedl, D. S. Lee, B. Krauss, L. Patthey, K. von Klitzing, J. H. Smet and U. Starke, 'Charge neutrality and band-gap tuning of epitaxial graphene on SiC by molecular doping', *Physical Review B*, 81 235401 (2010) http://link.aps.org/doi/10.1103/PhysRevB.81.235401

C. Lee Van Dover, D. Desbruyères, M. Segonzac, T. Comtet, L. Saldanha, A. Fiala-Medioni and C. Langmuir, 'Biology of the Lucky Strike hydrothermal field', *Deep Sea Research Part I: Oceanographic Research Papers*, 43 (9) (1996), 1509–29

D. C. Matthewson, R. J. van Aarde and J. D. Skinner, 'Population biology of house mice *(Mus musculus L.)* on sub-Antarctic Marion Island', *South African Journal of Zoology*, 29 (2) (1994), 99–106

D. Desbruyères, M. Biscoito, J-C. Caprais, A. Colaco, T. Comtet, P. Crassous, Y. Fouquet, A. Khripouno, N. Le Bris, K. Olu, R. Riso, P-M. Sarradin, M. Segonzaca and A. Vangriesheim, 'Variations in deep-sea hydrothermal vent communities on the Mid-Atlantic Ridge near the Azores plateau', *Deep Sea Research Part I: Oceanographic Research Papers*, 48 (2001), 1325–46

E. Kádár, A. Lobo-da-Cunha, R. S. Santos and P. Dando 'Spermatogenesis of *Bathymodiolus azoricus* in captivity matching reproductive behaviour at deep-sea hydrothermal vents', *Journal of Experimental Marine Biology and Ecology*, 335 (1) (2006), 19–26

E. Kádar, V. Costa and R. S. Santos, 'Distribution of micro-essential (Fe, Cu, Zn) and toxic (Hg) metals in tissues of two nutritionally distinct hydrothermal shrimps', *Science of the Total Environment*, 358 (1–3) (2006), 143–50

F. Gómez, E. Mateo-Martí, O. Prieto-Ballesteros, J. Martín-Gago and R. Amils, 'Protection of Chemolithoautotrophic bacteria exposed to simulated Mars environmental conditions', *Icarus*, 209 (2) (2010), 482–87

F-P. J. Martin, S. Rezzi, E. Peré-Trepat, B. Kamlage, S. Collino, E. Leibold, J. Kastler, D. Rein, L. B. Fay and S. Kochhar, 'Metabolic Effects of Dark Chocolate Consumption on Energy, Gut Microbiota, and Stress-Related Metabolism in Free-Living Subjects', *Journal of Proteome Research,* 8 (12) (2009), 5568–79

G. Yvon-Durocher, I. Jones, M. Trimmer, G. Woodward and J. M. Montoya, 'Warming alters the metabolic balance of ecosystems', *Philosophical Transactions of the Royal Society B: Biological Sciences*, 365 (1549) (2010), 2117–26

H. Jang, Y-K. Kim, S-R. Ryoo, M-H. Kim, D-H. Min, 'Facile Synthesis of Robust and Biocompatible Gold Nanoparticles', The Royal Society of Chemistry (2009) http://www.rsc.org/suppdata/CC/b9/b919971n/b919971n.pdf

J. Chen, 'Understanding depth variation of deep seismicity from *in situ* measurements of mineral strengths at high pressures', *Journal of Physics and Chemistry of Solids* 71 (8) (2010), 1032–37

J. R. Reeve, L. Carpenter-Boggs, J. P. Reganold, A. L. York, G. McGourty and L. P. McCloskey, 'Soil and Winegrape Quality in Biodynamically and Organically Managed Vineyards', *American Journal of Enology and Viticulture*, 56 (2005), 367–76

K. Duan, A. Tang and R. Wang, 'A new evaporation-based method for the preparation of biomimetic calcium phosphate coatings on metals', *Materials Science and Engineering C*, 29 (2009), 1334–37

Z-Y. Juang, C-Y. Wu, C-W. Lo, W-Y. Chen, C-F. Huang, J-C. Hwang, F-R. Chen, K-C Leou and C-H. Tsai, 'Synthesis of graphene on silicon carbide substrates at low temperature', *Carbon*, 47(8) (2009), 2026–31

L. De Pablo, M. Doval and A. La Iglesia, 'Geochemistry of reversible hydratable tephra from the Trans Mexican Volcanic Belt', *American Mineralogist*; 94 (11–12) (2009), 1603–15

L. I. Havelin, L. B. Engesæter, B. Espehaug, O. Furnes, S. A. Lie and S. E. Vollset, 'The Norwegian Arthroplasty Register 11 years and 73,000 arthroplasties', *Acta Orthopaedica Scandinavica*, 71 (4) (2000), 337–53

L. P. Chrysikoua and C. A. Samara, 'Seasonal variation of the size distribution of urban particulate matter and associated organic pollutants in the ambient air', *Atmospheric Environment*, 43(30) (2009), 4557–69

M. D. Askari, G. H. Miller and T. Vo-Dinh, 'Simultaneous detection of the tumor suppressor FHIT gene and protein using the multi-functional biochip' *Cancer Detection and Prevention Journal*, 26 (5) (2002), 33–42.

M. D. Holmes, W. Y. Chen, L. Li, , E. Hertzmark, D. Spiegelman and S. E. Hankinso, 'Aspirin Intake and Survival After Breast Cancer', *Journal of Clinical Oncology* 28 (9) (2010), 1467–72

M. Gonzalez-Rey, A. Serafim, R. Company and M. Joã Bebianno, 'Adaptation to metal toxicity: a comparison of hydrothermal vent and coastal shrimps Marine Ecology' 28 (1) (2007), 100–7

M. Gonzalez-Rey, A. Serafim, R. Company, T. Gomes and M. Joã Bebianno, 'Detoxification mechanisms in shrimp: comparative approach between hydrothermal vent fields and estuarine environments', *Marine Environmental Research*, 66 (1) (2008), 35–7

M. Kunowsky, B. Weinberger, F. Lamari Darkrim, F. Suárez-García, D. Cazorla-Amoro´s and A. Linares-Solano, 'Impact of the carbonisation temperature on the activation of carbon fibres and their application for hydrogen storage', *International Journal of Hydrogen Energy*, 33 (12) (2008), 3091–95

M. Kunowsky, J. P. Marco-Lozar, D. Cazorla-Amoro´s and A. Linares-Solano, 'Scale-up activation of carbon fibres for hydrogen storage', *International Journal of Hydrogen Energy*, 35 (6) (2010), 2393–402

M. S. Henry, J. J. Childress and D. Figueroa, 'Metabolic rates and thermal tolerances of chemoautotrophic symbioses from Lau Basin hydrothermal vents and their implications for species distributions', *Deep Sea Research Part I: Oceanographic Research Papers*, 55 (5) (2008), 679–95

P. Sandy, A. Ventura and T. Jacks, 'Mammalian RNAi: a practical guide', *Biotechniques*, 39 (2) (2005), 215–24

P. Sebastiani, N. Solovieff, A. Puca, S. W. Hartley, E. Melista, S. Andersen, D. A. Dworkis, J. B. Wilk, R. H. Myers, M. H. Steinberg, M. Montano, C. T. Baldwin and T. T. Perls, 'Genetic Signatures of Exceptional Longevity in Humans', *Science*, (2010), DOI: 10.1126/science.1190532 http://www.sciencemag.org/cgi/content/abstract/science.1190532

R. B. Pearson and B. E. Kemp, 'Chemical modification of lysine and arginine residues in the myosin regulatory light chain inhibits phosphorylation', *BBA - Biochimica et Biophysica Acta*, 870(2) (1986), 312–19

R. Company, A. Serafim, M. J. Bebianno R Cosson, B. Shillito and A. Fiala-Médioni, 'Effect of cadmium, copper and mercury on antioxidant enzyme activities and lipid peroxidation in the gills of the hydrothermal vent mussel *Bathymodiolus azoricus*', *Marine Environmental Research*, 58 (2–5) (2004), 377–81

R. Company, H. Felícia, A. Serafim, A. J. Almeida, M. Biscoito and M. J. Bebianno, 'Metal concentrations and metallothionein-like protein levels in deep-sea fishes captured near hydrothermal vents in the Mid-Atlantic Ridge off Azores', *Deep Sea Research Part I: Oceanographic Research Papers*, 57 (7) (2010), 893–908

R. de la Torre, L. G. Sancho, G. Horneck, A. de los Ríos, J. Wierzchos, K. Olsson-Francis, C. S. Cockell, P. Rettberg , T. Berger, J-P. P. de Vera, S. Ott, J. Martínez-Frías, P. Gonzalez-Melendi , M. M. Lucas, M. Reina, A. Pintado and R. Demets, 'Survival of lichens and bacteria exposed to outer space conditions – Results of the Lithopanspermia experiments', *Icarus*, 208 (2) (2010), 735–48

R.D. Gupta, 'A Review : Supercritical Fluid Extraction Technology', *Pharmainfo.net*, (2008) http://www.pharmainfo.net/reviews/review-supercritical-fluid-extraction-technology

R.M. Pilliar, 'Cementless implant fixation – toward improved reliability', *Orthopedic Clinics of North America* 36 (1) (2005), 113–9

S. Buscemi, S. Verga, J. A. Batsis, M. Donatelli, M. R. Tranchina, S. Belmonte, A. Mattina, A. Re and G. Cerasola, 'Acute effects of coffee on endothelial function in healthy subjects', *European Journal of Clinical Nutrition*, 64 (2010), 483–89

S. Eittreim, E. M. Thorndike and L. Sullivan, 'Turbidity distribution in the Atlantic Ocean', *Deep-Sea Research*, 23 (1976), 1115–27

S. Heyers, M. Sousa, O. Cangir, F. Schmoll, K. Schellander, H. van der Ven and M. Montag, 'Activation of mouse oocytes requires multiple sperm factors but not sperm PLCgamma1', *Molecular and Cellular Endocrinology*, 166 (1) (2000), 51–7

S. R. Paital and N. B. Dahotre, 'Calcium phosphate coatings for bio-implant applications: Materials, performance factors, and methodologies', *Materials Science and Engineering: R: Reports*, 66 (1–3) (2009), 1–70

S.R. Radin and P. Ducheyne, 'Plasma spraying induced changes of calcium phosphate ceramic characteristics and the effect on *in vitro* stability', *Journal of Materials Science: Materials in Medicine*, 3 (1) (1992), 33–42

T. A. Hilder and J. M. Hill, 'Modeling the Loading and Unloading of Drugs into Nanotubes', *Small*, 5(3) (2009), 300–8

T. K. Berthoud, H. A. Fletcher, D. Porter, F. Thompson, A. V. S. Hill, S. M. Todryk, 'Comparing human T cell and NK cell responses in viral-based malaria vaccine trials' *Vaccine*, 28 (1) (2009), 21–7

T. K. Berthoud, S. J. Dunachie, S. Todryk, A. V. S. Hill and H. A. Fletcher, 'MIG (CXCL9) is a more sensitive measure than IFN-γ of vaccine induced T-cell responses in volunteers receiving investigated malaria vaccines', *Journal of Immunological Methods*, 340 (1) (2009), 33–41

T. M. Alvesa and S.D.N. Lourenço, 'Geomorphologic features related to gravitational collapse: Submarine landsliding to lateral spreading on a Late Miocene–Quaternary slope (SE Crete, eastern Mediterranean)', *Geomorphology*, 123(1–2) (2010), 13–33

T. Quentina, A. Poppea, K. Bära, A. Siglerb, R. Fotha, I. Michel-Behnkec, T. Paula, M. Siglera, 'A novel method for processing resin-embedded specimens with metal implants for immunohistochemical labelling', *Acta Histochemica*, 111 (2009) 538–42

T. Zhang, W. P. Walawender and L. T. Fan, 'Grain-based activated carbons for natural gas storage', *Bioresource Technology*, 101 (6) (2010), 1983–91

V.G. Tarasov, A.V. Gebruk, A.N. Mironov and L.I. Moskalev, 'Deep-sea and shallow-water hydrothermal vent communities: two different phenomena?', *Chemical Geology*, 224 (1–3) (2005), 5–39

W. L. Nicholson and A. C. Schuerger, '*Bacillus subtilis* Spore Survival and Expression of Germination-Induced Bioluminescence After Prolonged Incubation Under Simulated Mars Atmospheric Pressure and Composition: implications for Planetary Protection and Lithopanspermia', *Astrobiology*, 5 (4) (2005), 536–44

Y. Yang, K-H Kim and J. L. Ong, 'A review on calcium phosphate coatings produced using a sputtering process – an alternative to plasma spraying', *Biomaterials*, 26 (3) (2005), 327–37

Photo acknowledgements

The publishers are grateful to the following for permission to reproduce copyright photographs and material:
Key: l = left, c = centre, r = right, t = top, b = bottom

Alamy ©Custom Medical Stock Photo for p19(l), ©Hunstock for p40, ©Dynamic Light USA for p54 (t), ©Keith Morris for p78(t), ©Charlie Lim for p88, ©Interfoto for p82(t), ©Stan Gamester for p82(cb), ©Steve Turner for p82(b); **Bloomsbury** for cover of *Aspirin* by Diarmuid Jeffreys – Reprinted by permission; **Bureau International des Poids et Mesures** for p50; **Cambridge University Press** for p14(f), p77; **CambridgeSoft.com** for p45; **Custom Medical Stock Photo** for p19(r); **Deep Sea Photography .com**/©Peter Batson for p54(rt); **Education Photos** ©John Walmsley for p6(b); **Getty Images** ©Keith Brofsky for p6 (t & inset); **istockphoto** ©zhang bo for p7, ©anti kainen for p8(br), ©zhang bo for p12, ©Oleg Prikhodko for p14(a), ©Paul Maguire for p17, ©Niko Guido for p19(c), ©L Calek for p22 (snail shell), ©Michael Steden for p26(br), ©dra_schwartz for p30 (mouse), ©Reimar Barnstorf for p33(d), ©Albert Lozano for p33(f), ©Caziopeia for p75(b), ©Oleg Prikhodko for p82(ct); **Kingsview Optical** for p33(a); **Macmillan Publishers Ltd**: Nature for p14(b) – Reprinted by permission; **National Oceanic & Atmospheric Administration** ©National Institute of Water & Atmospheric Research for 54(rb); **New Scientist Magazine** for p14(e); **News International Syndication** for p14(c); **Photolibrary** ©Hill Street Studios for p16, ©Mark Webster for p22 (boxfish), ©Ariadne van Zandbergen for p28(b), ©Roger Eritja for p32, ©Yoav Levy for p33(h), ©Jaume Gual for p65, ©Upperhall for p75(c); **Science Photo Library** ©Solvin Zankl. Visuals Unlimited for p26(t), ©Power and Syred for p28(t), ©Health Protection Agency for p30(main), ©Martyn F Chillmaid for p33(e), ©Zephyr for p33(g), ©Laguna Design for p46, ©A J Photo for p49, ©Power and Syred for p54(rc), ©Medical RF.com for p78(c), ©Andy Crump, TDR, WHO for p78(b); **Shutterstock** ©Kurt De Bruyn for p8(tr), ©Noam Armonn for p22 (beetle), ©pamspix for p22 (termite mound), ©Roger De Marfa for p22 (mosquito), ©Sandra Kemppainen for p22 (plant leaves), ©Janelle Lugge for p30 (inset), ©Nomad_Soul for p33(b), ©Noel Powell, Schaumburg for p67, ©Diana Taliun for p75(t); **University of Warwick, Mobile Robotics** for p84. The photographs on p33(a) and p55 are copyright free.

Author acknowledgements

I would like to thank all the Cambridge University Press team who have been involved with *Cambridge English for Scientists* for their expert advice and guidance, particularly Nik White, Jeremy Day and Sally Cooke. I would also like to thank Bethany Cagnol for her useful feedback, past and present colleagues at Crown English, Auckland and the University of Canberra English Language Institute for their encouragement, and Jonathan Farrell for his help and support.

Publisher's acknowledgements

We would like to thank Marc Fiedler and his colleagues at the MRC (Medical Research Council) Laboratory of Molecular Biology, Hills Road, Cambridge CB2 0QH, UK for kindly inviting us to visit their laboratory and for providing an invaluable insight into the world of professional scientific research. For their reviews and comments on earlier versions of the material for *Cambridge English for Scientists*, we would like to thank the following people:

Dr Andrew Sugden of *Science* International (Journal of the American Association for the Advancement of Science);

PhD students from the Wellcome Trust Sanger Institute, Cambridge: Ankur Mutreja, Anna V. Protasio, Daniela Robles, Laura Deakin, Madushi Wanaguru, Miao He, Sabrina Calabrassi, Saeed Al Turki.

Designed and produced by eMC Design Ltd, www.emcdesign.co.uk

Audio production by Leon Chambers

Picture research by Hilary Luckcock

Proofreading by Marcus Fletcher

Cambridge English for … is a series of courses for different areas of English for Specific Purposes. Written by professionals, these short courses combine the best in ELT methodology with real professional practice. For more information about Business and Professional English titles from Cambridge University Press visit www.cambridge.org/elt/professional

Other titles in the series: